ERIE WRECKS WEST

A GUIDE TO SHIPWRECKS OF WESTERN LAKE ERIE

Georgann & Michael Wachter

Cover painting by Georgann Wachter

ISBN: 0-9661312-2-3

Published by **CorporateImpact**
Avon Lake, Ohio
e-mail: impact@kellnet.com

CONTENTS

CONTENTS

ACKNOWLEDGEMENTS

We could not have produced this book without the help and encouragement of a great many people. In particular, we wish to express our appreciation to

The Great Lakes Historical Society in Vermilion, Ohio and staff members:

Chris Gillchrist, Executive Director

Peg Bechtol, Carla LaVigne, Martha Long, Noelle McFarland, William O'Brien (former Executive Director), Linda Pansing, Bill Stark.

Historical Collections of the Great Lakes at Bowling Green State University and staff members:

Robert Graham, Director

Mark Barnes, Former Archivist, and Jay Martin, former staff member, now director of the Wisconsin Maritime Museum in Manitowoc.

Kent Divers Association, Chatham, Ontario

Save Ontario Shipwrecks Windsor, Ontario

Many friends and dive partners provided significant encouragement and information. Especially helpful were:

Al Hart, provided access to his extensive collection of Great Lakes shipping information.

Ed & Rikki Herndendorf, verified information and provided survey data on several wrecks.

Mary & Larry Howard, have done some of the most extensive original research on Lake Erie shipwrecks.

Bill Kaman & Greg Millinger, conducted side scan surveys of many sites and permitted us to publish them.

Allan King, shared extensive knowledge on the locations and history of the shipwrecks surrounding Point Pelee.

Gary Kozak, gave us information on several sites he discovered using side scan sonar equipment.

C. Patrick Labadie, author, researcher, historian, offered photos, invaluable information and confirmation or rejection of some of our shipwreck identifications.

Jim Paskert, researcher, historian, provided information on the locations and identification of several shipwrecks

Roy Pickering, shared information, paintings, and research on the locations and history of the many shipwrecks.

Ralph Roberts, provided rare photos from his extensive private collection.

Dave & Annette Soule, our dive partners and fellow research enthusiasts are always there with research and moral support.

We also received information and assistance from the following individuals and institutions: Jennifer McLeod of Marsh Collection Society, Amherstberg, Ontario; Matthew Daley, Father Edward J. Dowling Marine Historical Collection, University of Detroit Mercy Library; John Polacsek, Dossin Great Lakes Museum, Detroit, Michigan; Rocky River Public Library, Rocky River, Ohio; Erie County Historical Society, Erie Pennsylvania; Great Lakes Marine and U.S. Coast Guard Memorial Museum, Ashtabula, Ohio; Rutherford B. Hayes Memorial Presidential Center, Freemont, Ohio; Western Lake Erie Historical Society, Toledo, Ohio; Gerry and Walter Paine, Avon Lake, Ohio.

DISCLAIMER

The authors have made every effort to assure the accuracy of the contents of this book. However, no warrantee is expressed or implied that the information contained in this volume is accurate or correct. In fact we expect to hear from many people pointing out errors in our facts! The authors shall in no way be responsible for any consequential, incidental, or exemplary loss or damage resulting from the use of any of the graphics or printed information contained in this book. The authors disclaim any liability for omissions, errors, or misprints and give notice to all readers that this book is not to be used for dive planning or navigation.

INTRODUCTION

We first published **Erie Wrecks, A Divers Guide** in April of 1997. Since that time, our research has been able to determine the identity of several previously unnamed wrecks, and many new shipwrecks have been found. Largely because of **Erie Wrecks, A Diver's Guide**, we have been fortunate to connect with many people who share our interest in the diving and learning about the heritage of the vessels on the lake floor. In this book we pass along new information about each shipwreck covered in the original Erie Wrecks and have added new shipwrecks not previously known. We have added GPS coordinates and many new photographs and drawings. Between **Erie Wrecks West** and **Erie Wrecks East** (published April 2000), we have covered approximately 200 Lake Erie Shipwrecks. When one recognizes there are a possible 4000 major ship losses in Lake Erie, our task will never be complete. But, rest assured, we'll keep trying.

The lure of a shipwreck is like no other for a diver. As you descend, you leave the present behind and enter a moment in the past. While you explore this unique time capsule, many questions go through your mind. What happened on the fateful day the ship went down? What was she carrying? Did the passengers and crew survive? This book and the companion volume, **Erie Wrecks East**, provide the answers to these questions for many of Lake Erie's shipwrecks.

As we began researching the shipwrecks we dive, we were impressed by the poignancy of news articles about a loss at sea. Typical of the pathos is the following article from the December 3, 1874, *Painesville Telegraph*:

MARINE.
A Terrible Lake Disaster

Monday afternoon J. M. Benjamin received a telegram from Geneva announcing the coming ashore at that point of the scow Pearl of Fairport, with two frozen bodies aboard. The vessel was owned and sailed by Captain E. A. Dayton of this place. The Pearl left Port Huron on the 18th, laden with 30,000 feet of lumber. The following day she was observed passing down the river, since which time nothing was heard or seen of her until she came ashore at daylight at the point above named. She beached about 50 to 70 feet from shore, when it was discovered that at least two persons were on board. No boat being at hand, recourse was had to the swimming out of a horse, when it was ascertained that the occupants were dead. A boat was afterward obtained, and the bodies, which proved to be those of a son of the captain, aged 12, and James Graham, aged 19, son of Captain George V. Graham, residing on the Headlands, were brought to shore.

Young Dayton was found lashed to the windlass, with all his clothes washed away except on those parts of the body where the rope bound them to him. In one of the pockets, which was held by the rope, were some papers belonging to his father, and a wallet containing a few dollars belonging to young Graham, which, it is supposed were placed in his keeping when made fast to the windlass. His body was completely encased in solid ice.

Young Graham was found sitting upright on the deck with his feet in the hold, both hands firmly grasping the edge of the deck on either side of him. He had on two suits of clothes, an oilcloth coat, a cap and mittens. He also was encased in ice.

Nothing is yet known of the fate of Captain Dayton, but the supposition is that he was washed overboard with the lumber on deck, all of which had disappeared. It is thought that the Pearl lost her spars in the gale of the 23rd and from that time till she came ashore, was drifting about, waterlogged, the sport of the wind and the waves. Capt. Dayton was in the prime of life, a much esteemed and respected citizen. The terrible sad fate of himself and son, and young Graham, is a deep affliction to their families, and elicits the warmest sympathies of their friends and the public generally.

There was no insurance on either the vessel or cargo. The loss of Messrs. Woodman and Branch, owners of the lumber, is not large, only the deck portion of the cargo being lost.

We have included many similar articles in this book.

The best protection our shipwreck heritage can have is an informed diver who respects the history of the vessel. We encourage the reader to learn more of the wrecks we dive and the events surrounding their loss.

Lake Erie is the fourth largest of the five Great Lakes by surface area but the smallest in volume. This shallow freshwater sea averages only 60 feet in depth though there is an area off of Long Point that is 210 feet deep. While her shallowness makes Lake Erie ideal for scuba diving, she is also the quickest to turn from millpond to white water fury. Many a ship was sent to the bottom by sudden squalls. Collisions and groundings in crowded, shallow Pelee Passage and off Long Point resulted in many more ship losses.

We have visited most of the shipwreck sites in this volume, and recorded our own observations and LORAN or DGPS numbers. LORAN numbers may soon be made obsolete by Global Positioning Systems. Where we have provided DGPS coordinates, anyone using a GPS should be able to go directly to the wreck. Where we have provided LORAN coordinates (TDs), recognize that LORAN numbers will vary by machine and location on the wreck charted, so you should bring several search markers to aid in locating the wreck. If we have only provided a position approximate (PA), we have not had our boat on the wreck and the coordinates should be considered a starting position for search purposes.

Our descriptions of the wreck sites are generally from personal experience. We have observed that over the years wrecks change and further deteriorate. Features are obscured by silting, storms and zebra mussels. As an example, at one time divers could swim under the windlass deck area of the schooner *Dundee*. One spring we returned to this site to find this forward area had collapsed. It was a sobering thought that divers could have been penetrating the wreck when the supports gave way.

Canada and the United States have laws prohibiting salvage without permits or the destruction of wreck sites.

Take care and good diving!

WRECK MAP

1 Marquette & Bessemer #2
2 Merida
3 Barr, H.A.
4 Raphael
5 Queen of the West
6 Lamb, L.L.
7 Olive Branch
8 North Carolina
9 Griffith, G.P.
10 Cleveco
11 Colgate
12 Sternless

13 Morpeth Schooner
14 Lycoming
15 Erieau Quarry Stone
16 Robert
17 Colonial
18 Fleetwood (Brick Wreck)
19 Vigor, Frank E.
20 Valentine
21 Little Wissahickon
22 Meyer, F.A.
23 Gale, Stephen F.
24 Luedtke, Duke

25 Dundee
26 Admiral
27 Algeria
28 Davis, Charles H.
29 Jones, Fannie L.
30 Wilson, Mabel
31 117 Street Wreck
32 Cleveland, H.G.
33 Griffin, John B.
34 Mecosta
35 Two Fannies
36 Bay Coal Schooner

37 Murphy, Paddy
38 Sand Merchant
39 Pridgeon, John Jr.
40 Craftsman
41 Ivanhoe
42 Alva B
43 Penelope
44 Colonel Cook
45 CEI Barge
46 Hickory Stick
47 Sheldon, Sarah
48 Saint Lawrence

48 Quito
49 Cascade
50 Morning Star
51 Wayne, Anthony
52 Cortland
53 Butters Marshall F.
54 Civil War Wreck
55 Willis
56 Gilbert, E.K. (Bow Cabin)
57 Net Wreck
58 Clarion
59 New Brunswick

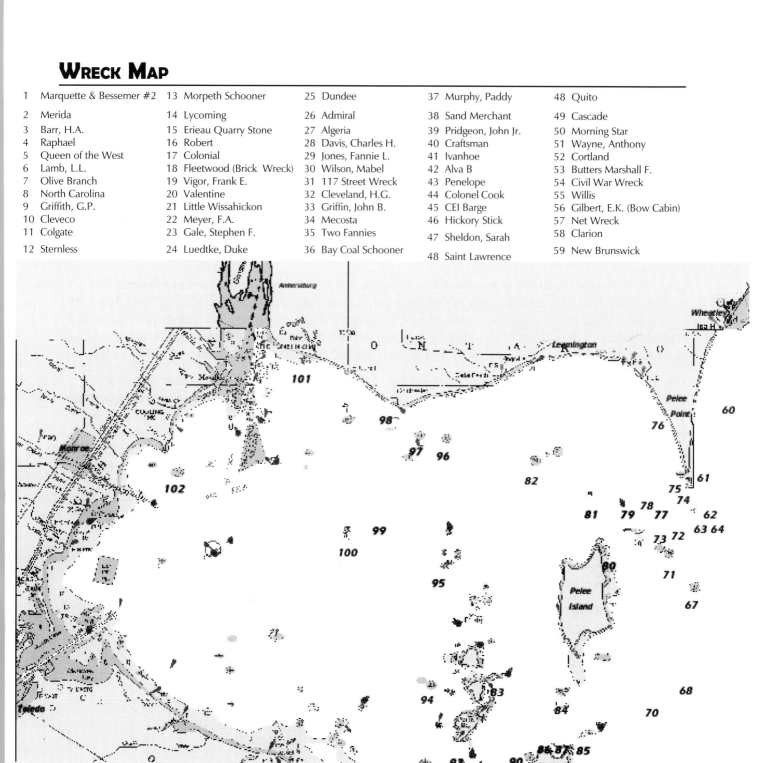

84 Keepsake
85 Saint Loius
86 Adventure
87 Hanna, W.R.
88 Prince, F.H.
89 Exchange
90 Relief
91 Mosher, Amareta
92 Spademan, Charles
93 Success
94 Toledo
95 Case (J.C. Lockwood)

96 Worthington, George
97 Grand Traverse
98 Wilcox, M.I.
99 Magnet
100 Wesee
101 Filer, D.L.
102 Sigel, General Franz

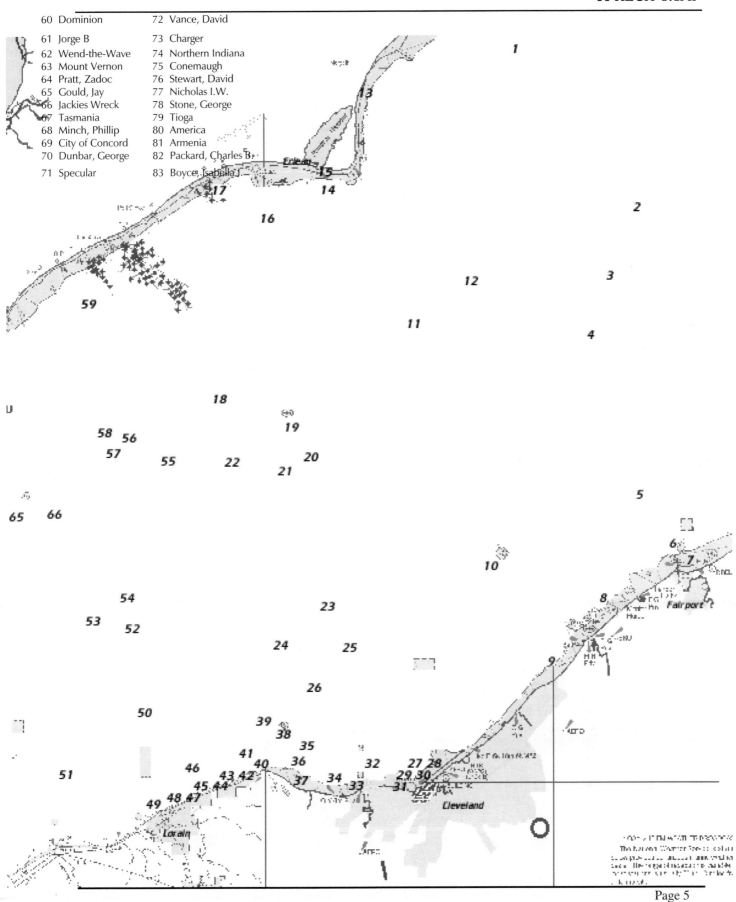

60 Dominion
61 Jorge B
62 Wend-the-Wave
63 Mount Vernon
64 Pratt, Zadoc
65 Gould, Jay
66 Jackies Wreck
67 Tasmania
68 Minch, Phillip
69 City of Concord
70 Dunbar, George
71 Specular

72 Vance, David
73 Charger
74 Northern Indiana
75 Conemaugh
76 Stewart, David
77 Nicholas I.W.
78 Stone, George
79 Tioga
80 America
81 Armenia
82 Packard, Charles B.
83 Boyce, Isabella J.

117TH STREET WRECK

Official #: unknown   **Site #:** 31

Location: 2.7 miles 276°T from Cleveland main harbor entrance

Coordinates: LORAN: 43771.9 57452.6   DGPS: 41 30.777   81 46.147

Lies: bow west   **Depth:** 40 feet

Type: tug   **Cargo:**

Power:

Owner(s)

Built:

Dimensions: **Tonnage:**

Date of Loss:

Cause of Loss: scuttled?

Tom Dowling

The tug Tom Dowling was typical of many early Great Lakes Towing Company vessels.
Great Lakes Historical Society

Story of the Loss:

Often, when the divers who discover a site have no idea what vessel they have found, the wreck is given a convenient nickname. The name, "117th Street Wreck", reflects the fact that this site is off Cleveland's west side. This small vessel probably dates from the late 1800's to early 1900's. During the late 1800's, the Great Lakes Towing Company scuttled a number of vessels that were no longer fit for service. We believe this wreck is one of these former Great Lakes Towing Company tugs.

The Wreck Today:

The wreck lies on a hard packed mud bottom in 40 feet of water. The port bow is semi-intact and a metal box-like structure lies in her bow. Many crock pieces and ceramic electrical parts have been found at this site. Off the main body is significant debris, including a metal ladder and pulley wheels. Her boiler is also present but it lies well off the main wreck.

This blue and white enamel coffee pot was recovered from the wreck site in the mid 1970's.

ADMIRAL

Official #: 222239

Site #: 26

Location: 10.6 miles 352°T from Rocky River, Ohio

Coordinates: LORAN: 43808.9 57412.7

DGPS: 41 38.244 81 54.197

Lies: bow south

Depth: 75 feet

Type: tug

Cargo: tanker barge *Cleveco*

Power: 800 horsepower steam engine

Owner(s) Cleveland Tankers, Inc. of Cleveland, Ohio

Built: 1922 at Manitowoc, Wisconsin

Dimensions: 93.3' x 22.1' x 11.7'

Tonnage: 130 gross   88 net

Date of Loss: Wednesday, December 2, 1942

Cause of Loss: storm

Admiral
Remickk Collection

Story of the Loss:

The *Admiral* left Toledo, Ohio at 2:45 p.m. Tuesday, December 1, 1942. She carried a crew of fourteen and towed the 260 foot tanker barge Cleveco loaded with one million gallons of fuel oil. On December 2, the vessels encountered a severe storm. According to the court proceedings following the incident; the *Cleveco*, by reason of steering gear trouble, had sheared off and had the *Admiral* about five points on her starboard bow. This sheer required releasing the strain on the towing cable to give the *Admiral* a chance to run freely until the *Cleveco* was again brought under control. The tug apparently disappeared between the time the master of the *Cleveco* first saw that the tug was in this position and the time it took him to get over to the lever to release the strain on the towing cable. About 4:00 a.m., *Cleveco's* Captain, William H. Smith, radioed for help when watchmen on the barge could not see the *Admiral's* lights and noticed the towline to the *Admiral* had dropped into the water.

Assuming the barge to be anchored to the sunken tug, the crew of the *Cleveco* cut her free. By 6:30 a.m. the winds were 70 miles per hour and the waves were running 18 feet. For almost 30 hours, rescue boats attempted to find the *Cleveco*. The strong winds and driving snow, which made it impossible for search ships to find the drifting tanker barge, eventually took the *Cleveco* and her crew of 18 to their doom off Euclid, Ohio.

The Wreck Today:

Located in 1969 by diver George Walton, the *Admiral* sits upright in 75 feet of water. While many artifacts, including the bell and all pilothouse equipment, have been removed, the vessel is essentially intact. The crew quarters and galley are silted in. The pilothouse and engine room may be penetrated with caution. The stack lies against the port side gunnel amidships. At one time the name was clearly legible on the bow, however, zebra mussels now cover the bow and obscure the name. Over the years, the *Admiral* has continued to sink. When first discovered her stern was well above the bottom of the lake. Today, the stern is almost entirely silted over.

There is no evidence of the towline being fowled in the prop. The position of the wreck indicates she went down stern heavy. This supports the theory that ice accumulating on the stern caused the tug to sink under the weight of ice and water as a wave overtook her.

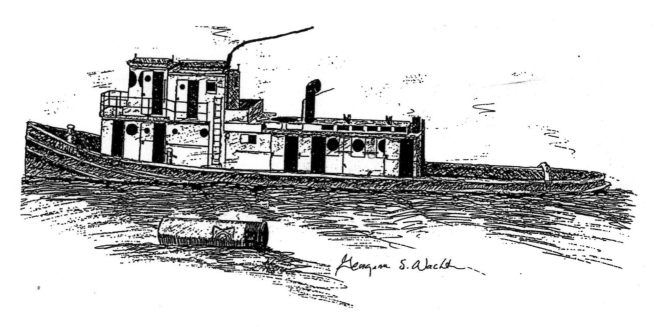

Admiral as she lays on the bottom
drawing by Georgann Wachter

Artifact Display

The Great Lakes Historical Society Museum in Vermilion, Ohio displays *Admiral* artifacts including her bell and a tool box filled with tools. The bell bears her former name, *W.H. Meyer*.

ADVENTURE

Official #:	105567	**Site #:**	86
Location:	North Bay of Kelleys Island		
Coordinates:	LORAN: 43688.1 57000.9	DGPS: 41 37.085 82 40.867	
Lies:	bow east	**Depth:**	10 feet
Type:	propeller	**Cargo:**	lime
Power:	steam		
Owner(s)	J.M. Robinson of Lorain, Ohio and Fred Groch of Sandusky, Ohio		
Built:	1875 at Detroit, Michigan by John Oades		
Dimensions:	108′ x 24′ x 8′3″	**Tonnage:**	148.97 gross 141.53 net
Date of Loss:	October 7, 1903		
Cause of Loss:	fire		

Adventure
Great Lakes Historical Society

Story of the Loss:

Originally built as a schooner measuring 104′ x 24′ x 8′, the *Adventure* was converted to steam power by Henry D. Root at Sandusky, Ohio in 1897. At the time of her loss, she measured 108′ x 24′ x 8′3″.

Having traveled from Sandusky to Kelleys Island under command of Captain John Lowes, the *Adventure* had moored at the Kelleys Island Lime and Transport Company's North Bay Dock and taken on a load of lime. While lying at the dock, the *Adventure* caught fire in the hold forward of the boiler. In order to save the schooner *Anderson*, which was moored nearby, Captain Regan of the tug *Smith* quickly towed the blazing propeller away from the dock. Captain John Lowes, his wife, young daughter, and crew were all saved from the fire. News reports of the day indicate that the crew was fortunate to escape with their lives.

The Wreck Today:

The *Adventure* sits on a sand and rock bottom only 100 feet from shore. You'll see some machinery, her drive shaft, and hull structure perpendicular to the shore straight out from the two large round boulders half way up the eastern peninsula. Since our first printing, the propeller was returned to the site from the Heath, Ohio street department scrap pile. The wreck of the scow *W.R. Hanna* (tentative identification) lies 40 feet north of the *Adventure's* stern, parallel to shore. With the clear shallow water, this location becomes heavily covered in weeds at times in the late summer.

CAUTION: Watch for heavy boat traffic. And, be careful not to run your boat aground.

Kelleys Island

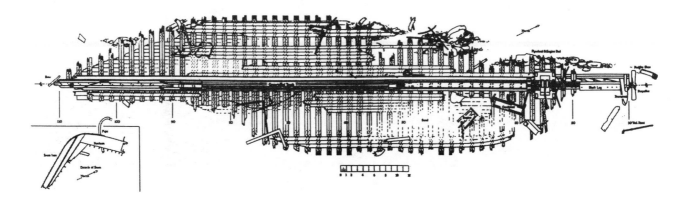

Site survey conducted by Field School in Nautical Archiology, September 5-9, 1997, Firelands Campus, Bowling Green State University.
Drawing by C. Patrick Labadie.

ALGERIA

Official #: 107222   **Site #:** 27

Location: 1 mile north of Cleveland Harbor, Ohio

Coordinates: LORAN: 43783.6 57482.2   DGPS: 41 31.225   81 42.944

Lies: east - west   **Depth:** 40 feet

Type: schooner / barge   **Cargo:** iron ore

Power: sail

Owner(s) William Sluemmer of Mt. Clemens, Michigan

Built: 1896 at West Bay City, Michigan by James Davidson

Dimensions: 288'7" x 44'6" x 19'1"   **Tonnage:** 2033.66 gross 1917.68 net

Date of Loss: Wednesday, May 9, 1906

Cause of Loss: foundered in storm

Algeria
Historical Collections of the Great Lakes

Story of the Loss:

A longshoremen's strike was in full force when the *Algeria* arrived at Cleveland on May 8, 1909. She was forced by the strike to remain at anchor outside the harbor. Four of her crew went ashore Tuesday evening in the schooner's only boat. Their planned return at 10:00 p.m. was prevented by stormy waters. When the storm warnings were raised atop the Society of Savings Bank, the big steamers came inside the breakwater, but the sailing vessels could not enter.

At 2:00 a.m. Wednesday, a distress rocket was launched from the deck of the *Algeria*. This attracted the attention of the Cleveland lifesaving crew and the steamer *L.C. Hanna*. Prevented by the rough water from getting to the *Algeria*, the *Hanna* circled the stricken schooner for two hours. Finally, the *Hanna* was able to reach the cook, Thomas Sullivan, with a rescue line, hauling him, more dead than alive, to safety.

Having worked heroically against the raging sea, the lifesaving boat reached the *Algeria* at 4:00 a.m. and found nothing remaining but her masts above the water. However, to the good fortune of the crew of the schooner *Iron Queen*, the lifeboat was nearby when they began to founder. All of the *Iron Queen's* crew was saved by the lifesaving crew.

Captain Matthew Elner and Engineer George Wallon lost their lives when the *Algeria* went down. Charles Johnson, a seaman on the *Algeria*, reported, "Our coming on shore on Tuesday afternoon was really the cause of the death of Captain Elner. We took the only boat the barge possessed and it was, therefore, impossible for the others to leave the craft when they finally found it was sinking."

The Wreck Today:

The *Algeria* lies slightly to the east of the Cleveland Harbor entrance. She has been reduced to a pile of wood with ships knees and cable strewn along her flattened hulk. Heavy commercial and pleasure boat traffic make this a tricky dive.

ALVA B

Official #:	106738	**Site #:**	42
Location:	1 mile west of Avon Point, Ohio approximately 100 yards off shore		
Coordinates:	LORAN: 43733.1 57314.6	DGPS: 41 30.768 82 01.894	
Lies:	bow east	**Depth:**	12 feet
Type:	tug	**Cargo:**	none
Power:	steam		
Owner(s)	John Freitus of Buffalo, New York — formerly Great Lakes Towing Company		
Built:	1890 at Buffalo, New York		
Dimensions:	73'6" x 18'5" x 10'6"	**Tonnage:**	83 gross
Date of Loss:	Thursday, November 1, 1917		
Cause of Loss:	ran aground in storm		

Alva B
Historical Collections of the Great Lakes

Story of the Loss:

The *Alva B* is noted for searching for the *Clarion* when she burned off of Southeast Shoal on December 8, 1909. Thirteen men from the *Clarion* were believed to have escaped in an open lifeboat. All hope of finding them was abandoned when the *Alva B* steamed into Cleveland completely covered with ice. She reported finding no trace of the wreckage, boat, or crew of the *Clarion*.

According to her Captain Barrington, the *Alva B* was en route from Sandusky, Ohio to Cleveland to be turned over to the Army Corps of Engineers for government service when she encountered a gale. She sprung a leak in the storm shortly after passing Lorain Harbor. "We used two siphons to pump out the water but were soon working in water up to our waists." The crew reports an attempt was made to beach the tug before abandoning her. Another story has it that the captain liked to warm his innards on a regular basis. The drinks were on him when the tug stopped in Huron and he was moved by the spirits to stop again in Lorain. As they approached Avon Lake, the crew was drunk and mistook the lights of Beach Park Amusement Park for Cleveland Harbor. The tug turned hard to the south and ran for the lights. She ran aground just east of Beach Park and damaged the wooden hull beyond repair. The storm followed, ensuring the total loss of the vessel.

Either way, six crewmen, including owner John Freitus, abandoned the tug and took to a small boat. Before they reached the safe shores of Avon Point, the *Alva B* had sunk to the bottom.

The Wreck Today:

The *Alva B* sits upright in only 12 feet of water. With her stern to the west, the boiler is off the boat to the east of the prop shaft. Large fish are attracted to the wreck and congregate around the boiler and wooden planking. In 1970 the ships 8 foot anchor and some chain were recovered by a group of local residents and placed at the Aqua Marine Resort in Avon Lake. In October of 1989 the 7 ' 3", 2390 pound prop was removed and donated to Miller Road Park in Avon Lake, Ohio.

Boaters beware! The boiler rises to within 3 feet of the surface. One unsuspecting dive boat was using a Westmar scanning sonar to locate the wreck. Although the wreck did not show up on the sonar, the divers found the wreck when they struck the boiler with the sonar head.

The Alva B's propeller is on display at Miller Road Park in Avon Lake, Ohio

Author Mike Wachter examines the Alva B's anchor, on display at Aqua Marine Resort in Avon Lake, Ohio.

AMERICA

Official #:   **Site #:**   80

Location: northeast tip Pelee Island ½ mile below lighthouse

Coordinates: LORAN: 43783.5   57078.4   DGPS: 41 49.675 82 38.066

Lies: scattered   **Depth:**   15 feet

Type: sidewheel steamer   **Cargo:**   passengers and package freight

Power: two 600 hp vertical beam engines with 32' diameter sidewheels

Owner(s)   David S. Bennett, 1853-1854; Lysander M. Cushings *et al*, 1852-53; John R. Philips, 1848-52, all of Buffalo, New York

Built: 1847 at Port Huron, Michigan by John W. Serles

Dimensions: 240'2" x 34'2" x 13'8"   **Tonnage:**   1083 gross

Date of Loss: Wednesday, April 5, 1854

Cause of Loss: ran aground

America
Family of Eric Heyl

Story of the Loss:

Advertised as "built with direct reference to safety" and "lighted with Solar Gas," *America* spent seven mishap filled years carrying passengers and package freight on the Buffalo to Sandusky and Buffalo to Chicago runs. On July 31,1850, she burst a steam pipe, killing eight passengers, three crewmen and scalding 30 others. On July 12, 1852, while en route from Cleveland to Buffalo, *America* struck the bow of the propeller *City of Oswego*, bounced off her and rammed her a second time, sending *Oswego* to the bottom with a loss of fifteen lives. In 1854, she holed herself on the rocks in Dunkirk Harbor, was scuttled, and later salvaged.

The *America* left Cleveland for Toledo April 5, 1854. After midnight, the captain went to bed, leaving the mate instructions to steer a specified course. Believing the captain to be mistaken, the mate steered a different course bringing the vessel too close to Pelee Island. Realizing his mistake, the mate awoke the captain in time for him to watch the hapless ship run aground 600 feet from Pelee Island Light.

As it was a calm night, *America* would have sailed again had tugs arrived in time. Unfortunately a northeaster kicked up the evening of April 7, and by the evening of April 8 there was nothing left to save. The crew was taken aboard the propeller *Granite State*, and the propeller *Bruce* carried the captain to Detroit.

The Wreck Today:

America lies on rock bottom in 15' of water. Her boiler is the most prominent remaining feature and it rises to within 2 feet of the surface. Northwest of the boiler is a section of bulkhead. Surrounding these large pieces are many planks, spikes, and lots of nice bass.

Caution to boaters: The GPS numbers above place you immediately over the boiler and there is scant clearance over her boiler.

America advertisement

ARMENIA

Official #: 107219   **Site #:** 81

Location: Pigeon Bay 10 miles northwest of Southeast Shoal

Coordinates: LORAN: 43806.6 57091.0   DGPS: PA: 41 52.95   82 38.51

Lies: bow north   **Depth:** 39 feet

Type: schooner/barge   **Cargo:** ore

Power: sail/towed

Owner(s) West Division Steam Ship Company

Built: 1896 at West Bay City, Michigan by James Davidson

Dimensions: 288'6" x 44'6" x 19'1"   **Tonnage:** 2040 gross 1919 net

Date of Loss: Wednesday, May 9, 1906

Cause of Loss: foundered in storm

Armenia
Historical Collections of the Great Lakes

Story of the Loss:

A fierce storm on Lake Erie was responsible for sinking five vessels in one day, two at Cleveland (the *Algeria* and the *Iron Queen*) and three in western Lake Erie (the *Wilcox*, the *Armenia*, and the scow

Algonia). The *Armenia* was being towed by the *Fred Pabst* when she foundered with no loss of life. Four months after the *Armenia* sank, the steamer *Charles B. Packard* struck her and went to the bottom.

From the Toledo Blade, May 10, 1906:

MARINE

MAY STORM WAS SERIOUS
Boats Wrecked and Several Lives Lost.

IRON QUEEN'S CLOSE CALL
Was Decks to When the Tugs Got the Craft
Inside the Harbor at Cleveland.

Four schooners and a scow were sunk in the gale Tuesday night which swept Lake Erie. They were the schooner Algeria, 1,917 tons; schooner Iron Queen, 1,321 tons; schooner Armenia, 1,919 tons; and the schooner M. I. Wilcox, 358 tons. The first two went down off Cleveland, and the other two near Colchester light. Capt. Martin Elner and George Wallon, of the Algeria, lost their lives.

The steamer L. C. Hanna, seeing the distress signals from the Algeria, went to the rescue and after spending two hours in circling the sinking schooner a line was finally thrown to Thomas Sullivan, the cook of the Algeria, and he was hauled aboard, more dead than alive.

The life-saving crew at Cleveland made an heroic attempt to save the men on the Algeria, but could find no one. The life-savers were successful, however, in taking off the crew of the Iron Queen. Five men of the steamer Algeria went ashore the evening before the storm, taking the only serviceable boat with them.

The Armenia and the M. I. Wicox were abandoned off Colchester light by their crews when it was found they would not weather the gale.

The Wreck Today:

This wreck was dynamited so it is widely scattered. At her bow you'll find many machinery parts and he rudder lies off the stern. This vessel is directly in the shipping lanes and a sharp lookout needs to be maintained. Watch for snagged nets.

H. A. Barr

Official #:   C 107489   **Site #:**   3

Location: in Canadian waters 30 miles north of Mentor, Ohio

Coordinates: LORAN: 44118.3 57803.2   DGPS: 42 09.111   81 23.414

Lies: bow northeast   **Depth:**   84 feet

Type: schooner / Barge   **Cargo:**   iron ore

Power: towed by Steamer *Theano*

Owner(s)   Algoma Central Steamship Lines, Sault St. Marie, Ontario

Built: 1893 by James Davidson, West Bay City, Michigan

Dimensions: 217′ x 35′ x 16′9″   **Tonnage:**   1119.59 gross 1063.62 net

Date of Loss: Wednesday, September 24, 1902

Cause of Loss: foundered in storm

H. A. Barr Windlass
Georgann Wachter

Story of the Loss:

Earlier in her career (1897) as a barge, in tow of the steamer *J.H. Outhwaite*, the *Barr* went aground at False Presque Isle Point, Lake Huron.

Under tow of the steamer *Theano*, the *H. A. Barr* left Lake Superior bound for Ohio ports with iron ore. As the vessels traversed Lake Erie, they battled a northeast gale that buffeted the ships with immense seas. Losing the battle with the gale, the *Barr* settled lower in the water until the seas were breaking over her deck. As the crew struggled to save her, giant breaking waves washed her hatch covers to sea. With her hatches open to the raging storm, the *Barr* was doomed. The crew abandoned her and took the lifeboats to the relative safety of the *Theano*. Drenched, but safe aboard the *Theano*, the crew of the *H. A.. Barr* watched helplessly as she settled to the bottom.

The Wreck Today:

The bow section of the wreck is upright in 80 feet of water. The stern is a pile of rubble encased in fish net. Although the port bow rail is broken the bow is largely intact. Zebra mussels cover the dead-eyes and belaying pins in their holders. Moving from the bow down the center line of the wreck one encounters the windlass, foremast, open hatch, capstan, winch, and mainmast before confronting the fish nets to the stern.

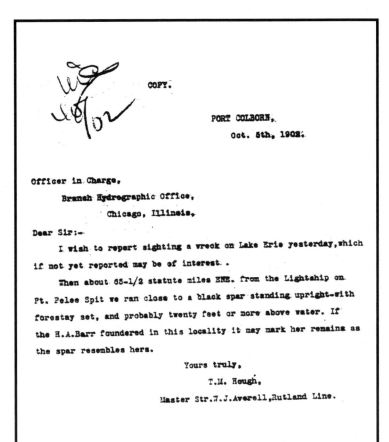

Letter reporting sighting of the wreck of the H. A. Barr
Author's Collection

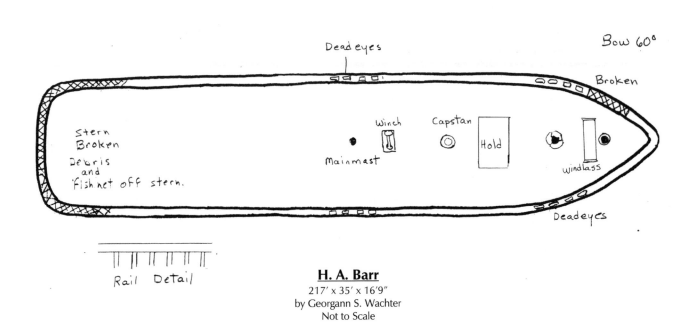

H. A. Barr
217' x 35' x 16'9"
by Georgann S. Wachter
Not to Scale

Bay Coal Schooner

Official #:

Location: four miles off Bay Village, Ohio

Coordinates: LORAN: 43764.5 57374.8

Lies: bow north

Type: scow

Power: sail

Owner(s)

Built:

Dimensions: 74'8" x 20-21'

Date of Loss: mid 1800's

Cause of Loss: fire?

Site #: 36

DGPS: 41 33.009 81 56.077

Depth: 55 feet

Cargo: coal

Tonnage:

Typical Two Masted Schooner
Merchant Vessels of the Great Lakes

Story of the Loss:

This two masted scow dates from the mid 1800's. We believe it to be the *Industry*, which sank in 1874.
The *Industry* was built in Port Rowan in 1848. She measured 71'6" x 17'6" x 5'6". On August 22, 1874,
a northeast wind was blowing as the *Industry* left Cleveland, Ohio. She carried a load of coal and was
approximately 10 miles off Lorain, Ohio when she suddenly took on water. Captain D. Dues and crew
abandoned the sinking scow and rowed for the Black River in the ships yawl boat . All arrived safely.

In conflict with this possibility are indications that this wreck may have had a fire on board.

A survey of the site conducted under the auspices of the Great Lakes Historical Society failed to definitively identify the ship.

The Wreck Today:

The wreck lays on a mud bottom with silt almost over the transom on the starboard side. The cross members are intact. There is no decking and the bow is broken. She has a square stern. Large timbers with iron parts may have supported the windlass. The vessel has a slight list to port.

Bay Coal Schooner
by Georgann S. Wachter
Not to Scale

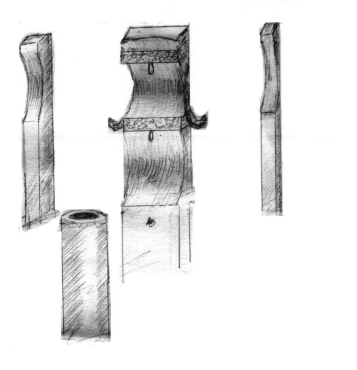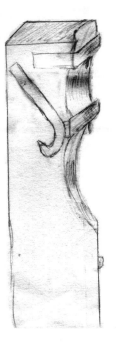

Detail of uprights

ISABELLA J. BOYCE

Official #: 100446   **Site #:** 83
Location: East Point Reef off Middle Bass Island
Coordinates: LORAN: 56972.2   43709.0   GPS: 41 41.830   82 46.505
Lies: scattered with the bow north   **Depth:** 4 to10 feet
Type: sandsucker   **Cargo:** None
Power: 425 HP fore & aft compound 19″ cylinder -32″x26″ stroke
Owner(s) Interlake Sand & Gravel Company
Built: 1889 at Manitowoc, Wisconsin by Burger & Burger
Dimensions: 138′ x 29′6″ x 11′   **Tonnage:** 368.28 gross   316.95 net
Date of Loss: Wednesday, June 6, 1917
Cause of Loss: grounded — fire

Isabella J. Boyce
Great Lakes Historical Society

Story of the Loss:

The sandsucker *Isabella J. Boyce* was bound from Cleveland to pick up a load of sand off Point Pelee when she went aground on East Point Reef at Middle Bass Island. After sounding distress signals, Captain William McFadden, went by launch to summon help in Put-in-Bay. The crew continued their efforts to free the grounded ship, until fire broke out above the engine. As the flames spread, the fish hatchery boat, *Oliver Perry* came to aid in fighting the flames. Unsuccessful in quelling the fire, Captain Pickforde of the *Oliver Perry*, assisted all 12 crewmen to land their lifeboats safely on South Bass Island at Put-in-Bay, Ohio.

Waves continued to pound on the grounded and charred vessel destroying much of what remained. Most of her machinery was purchased and salvaged by the Sun Manufacturing Company of Buffalo, New York.

The Wreck Today:

The charred, broken up remains of the *Boyce* lie widely scattered in shallow water on a rock bottom off the northeast tip of Middle Bass Island. The location provided puts you on her engine flywheel. The extensive debris field has pipes, metal support beams, wood frame members , and many small vessel parts.

CAUTION: A rock reef lies immediately inshore from this location. In low water the rocks are exposed or the water is breaking over them. Approaching from the north, there are large submerged boulders that can do some severe damage to your boat.

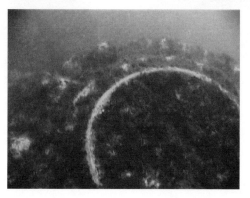

Engine parts are scattered at the Isabella J. Boyce site. Vidio capture by Mike Wachter.

MARSHALL F. BUTTERS

Official #:   91408   **Site #:**   53

Location: just north of the U.S., Canada border 15 miles north of Lorain, Ohio

Coordinates: LORAN: 43791.1 57233.0   DGPS: 41 43.636   82 17.370

Lies: bow north   **Depth:**   70 feet

Type: lumber hooker   **Cargo:**   lumber and shingles

Power: 375 hp steeple compound engine,17" cylinder, 40 x 36 stroke, made in Philadelphia by N. Leait. 18'8" x 13' boiler built in Ferrysburg, Michigan by Johnson Brothers in 1895

Owner(s)   Ludington Transfer Company

Built: 1882 at Milwaukee, Wisconsin by Milwaukee Shipyard Company

Dimensions: 164' x 30'4" x 10'5"   **Tonnage:**   376 gross 229.19 net

Date of Loss: Black Friday, October 20, 1916

Cause of Loss: foundered

Marshall F. Butters
Historical Collections of the Great Lakes

Story of the Loss:

Launched April 1, 1882, the *Marshall F. Butters* was the first ship on the Great Lakes with electric running lights. She was named for the son in a father & son owned logging railroad at Tallman, Michigan -- Butters, Peters, & Company. The firm liquidated in 1900.

Bound from the Georgian Bay for Cleveland with a load of lumber and shingles, the *Butters* ventured out of the Detroit River toward the Southeast Shoal Light into the beginnings of a storm. Unfortunately for the *Butters*, this was to be no ordinary storm. Also lost on Lake Erie that day were *the Merida,* the *Colgate,* and the *D.L. Filer*.

As the winds grew stronger the tiny lumber hooker shifted her load in the rising seas. Captain Charles McClure ordered the load trimmed. However, around noon, Chief Engineer Bert Randall discovered water rising in the bilges. McClure started the pumps and changed course for Lorain Harbor. As the ship sank lower in the water, the fire in her boilers was extinguished and the ship was doomed.

The *Butters* drifted at the mercy of the seas. Three crewmen stayed aboard to sound the distress signal while twelve of the crew took to the lifeboats. Captain F.B. Cody of the steamer *Frank R. Billings* could not hear the distress signal over the raging storm, but he could see the smoke billowing from the ill-fated vessel's whistle. Bringing his ship about in the heavy seas, he used storm oil to help get close enough to secure a rescue line to the sinking *Butters*. The *Frank R. Billings* pulled the three men to safety and carried them to Cleveland.

The *F. G. Hartwell* picked up the 12 men who escaped by lifeboat. Word of their safety was delayed by a day as the *Hartwell* sat out the storm unable to enter Fairport Harbor.

From the Detroit Free Press, October 21, 1916:

15 FACE DEATH WHEN GALE SINKS LUMBER SHIP IN LAKE ERIE

Marshall F. Butters Plunges to Bottom Off Detroit River

CREW BELIEVED SAVED: 3 LAND

Blizzard That Hits State Ends Her Ill-Starred Trip.

Cleveland, Oct. 20. — Fifteen men faced death in a losing battle against the fury of the elements on Lake Erie today, when the steamer Marshal F. Butters, carrying a cargo of lumber to Cleveland, foundered in a 50 mile gale while two other steamers stood by powerless to help.

The story of the shipwreck was brought to Cleveland by three of the survivors picked up by the ore carrier Frank Billings.

Whether any lives were lost will not be known until the steamer F. G. Hartwell, which is believed to have picked up the remainder of the crew, reaches Fairport tomorrow morning.

continued on next page

Storm Delays Rescue Ship

The heavy storm which rendered the efforts of the two larger steamers to save the Marshall F. Butters ineffectual, prevented the F. G. Hartwell from entering Fairport Harbor tonight. The Billings was delayed hours by the heavy seas under whose lash all lake craft fled to cover today.

Joseph Scheffenger, steward; Henry Raatz, fireman, and Neil Harrington, wheelsman, are the members of the crew of the doomed vessel who reached Cleveland tonight. They were the last to jump from the Butters as the ship sank 12 miles southeast of the Southeast shoal lightship near the mouth of the Detroit River.

Swept about helplessly in the trough of waves for hours, the Butters, a wooden vessel of comparatively light tonnage, was abandoned by her crew at 1:00 in the afternoon, after she had filled with water and lost part of her deck load.

Climax of Unlucky Voyage

The disaster was the climax of a voyage marked by mishap and hardship ever since the Butters left Midland, Ont. at Georgian Bay on Tuesday for Cleveland.

Water was discovered in the hold shortly after noon today by Bert Randall, the chief engineer. He informed Captain Charles E. McClure, who immediately ordered all the pumps put to work and changed his course for Lorain, O., which would have been a shorter run.

Despite the heroic efforts of the crew, the water gained in the hold. Distress signals were flown and the Billings and Hartwell went to the rescue. After much maneuvering, the Butters crew got away in small boats and the steamer sank.

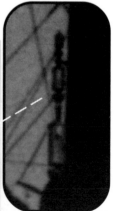

Profile of the Butters from the Remickk Collection with her unique triple whistle.

The Wreck Today:

The *Butters* lies north-south with the bow to the north. She sits upright with a slight list to starboard in 70 feet of water. The bow and stern are collapsed. The boiler, engine, and amidships section are largely intact. The capstan lies to the starboard side off the stern. Copper sheathing remains on the rudderpost. At the bow there is an anchor to starboard and the windlass is still in place. In 1999, a fishnet snagged on the starboard bow and further separated that side from the stem.

Pump on the wreck of the Marshall F. Butters.

Engine on the wreck of the Marshall F. Butters.

Boiler on the wreck of the Marshall F. Butters.

Video captures by Mike Wachter

CASCADE

Official #:	126913	**Site #:**	49

Location: 200 feet off the west breakwall at Lorain, Ohio
Coordinates: LORAN: 43693.0 57221.1   DGPS   PA: 41 28.55   82 11.50
Lies: scattered   **Depth:**   30 feet
Type: tug   **Cargo:**   light
Power: high pressure steam
Owner(s)   Elihu M. Pierce & Walter Wood, B&O Railroad, Cleveland, Ohio
Built: 1892 at Buffalo, New York by O'Grady & Maher
Dimensions: 73'5" x 19'8" x 10'5"   **Tonnage:**   77.28 gross   38.64 net
Date of Loss: Sunday, January 24, 1904
Cause of Loss: cut by ice

Cascade
Historical Collections of the Great Lakes

Story of the Loss:

Thirteen men set off on a mission to rescue 6 scows that had been swept out of the flooded Black River two days earlier and lodged at Avon Beach. The weather was blowing 50 mph from the northwest. Two men were put on the B&O fuel scow to secure her to the tug. As the winds increased and blew in ice flows, Captains Vosburg and Bowen decided to return to Lorain. The ice flows soon caused the *Cascade* to spring a leak as she pushed blindly through the snow. Captain Vosburg drove the tug into the thick field ice to prevent her from sinking.

Before leaving the stricken tug, the crew managed to remove a large bell, some brass railings, and the compass. Then, the men all got out and began to walk through the thick swirling snow. They soon found they were going in the wrong direction. One man fell through the ice but was rescued. Finally, all came ashore just west of the Lorain lighthouse.

<u>**From the Lorain Newspapers:**</u>

The Cascade, Worsted In Battle With Ice and Storm, Sank In Lake Erie Yesterday Afternoon

In the midst of the heavy gale and driving snow storm the tug with her thirteen plucky men aboard started down the lake toward Avon Beach, where the boats were reported. The gale was blowing fifty miles an hour. It was a cold and biting wind. The snow was cold, thick and penetrating, blinding all on board and obscuring from sight everything more than fifty feet away.

The trip to Beach Point was made with the howling gale behind. There the B. & O. fuel scow, four scows of Breyman Brothers and a Gaynor scow were adrift. The fuel scow was the nearest this way and the tug succeeded in reaching her. Two men were placed aboard of her with the Intention of putting her in shape to tow home. They built a fire and set to work preparing to make a line fast to the tug.

Then those on the tug discovered that the fierce northwest gale was increasing In force, driving huge floes of ice before it. The ice was fast closing in upon them and both Captains Vosburg and Bowen agreed that no further delay should be allowed, but that every effort should be made to get home. The two men on the scow were recalled, the tug put about and started for Lorain. By this time the storm had reached its height. The gale had increased, while the snow was practically impenetrable. To those in the pilothouse of the tug it seemed as though they were completely shut in, it being impossible to see a thing ahead of them.

They plowed on, unable to see the huge cakes of ice in their path, but wincing involuntarily as each new floe struck the staggering boat. They plunged ahead and were congratulating themselves that they must be near the port of home when a fireman reported that the hold was filling with water. It was siphoned out and the little tug still pushed on. But again the water gushed in to be once more siphoned out, and they still thought they were safe. For the third time a fireman reported that the hold was full of water. The engineer went forward to see for himself. He discovered then what was till then unsuspected. The water was pouring in just aft of the bow in torrents, gushing in much faster than they could hope to pump it out again. He returned to his engine, but, although the siphons worked to their capacity, the water soon reached the fire and all was over.

When It was found that nothing could be done Capt. Vosburg headed the tug straight into the thick field ice and wedged her into it. The men got off, while the wheel was then put hard aport. When every man was safely off, the tug swung around and backed off into clear water. Four times she swung around in a circle, then sank out of sight. Left alone on the Ice the men were in an unenviable plight. Cold, they were at the mercy of a fifty-mile gale, which made good use of its clear sweep of ice-covered lake to swirl around the little party in wild fury. The shore was shut out from view but they started off at random. On the way many slipped, fell on the ice and slid off considerable distance. The fierce wind made It almost impossible to keep on their feet. Harry Courtright fell through a treacherous piece of ice, but was rescued by his companions with the aid of a board. They soon found that they were going in the wrong direction and retraced their steps. They finally got ashore just west of the lighthouse.

Captains Voeburg and Bowen when seen this morning, told the following story regarding their experiences: The Cascade went east as far as a point about a mile east of the Avon powerhouse of the Lake Shore Electric line. Nearly all the way they were compelled to break through ice and drifts.. They had broken through the ice almost to the scows when the wind commenced blowing a gale in from the lake and the ice started to crowd in. They immediately turned about and started for home, fearing to be caught by the incoming ice. When they reached a point about a quarter of a mile off the end of the piers, near the site of the new breakwater and at a point north by northeast, the fireman announced that the boat was fast filling with water. The water soon reached the fire and of course there could be no steam generated. At once Captain Vosburg decided to head his boat for the Ice and get his crew off. Shortly after the crew got off the tug commenced to go round and went down a few minutes afterwards. Captain Bowen said it was impossible for the men to see her go down on account of the snow storm.

Captain Vosburg said the hole must have been made in the tug when they were working amongst the ice at Avon Point and that it is probable a piece of the ice plugged up the hole until they reached the point where the tug went down. He said that the hole was on the port side about two planks below the water line.

The Wreck Today:

A couple of pieces of wood and metal girders is all that marks the site of the *Cascade*. There is a hard packed mud bottom. Look for the many anchors fishermen have lost near the breakwall and watch for heavy boat traffic.

CASE

Official #:	C-126198	**Site #:**	95

Location: 600 feet off shore southwest side of East Sister Island

Coordinates: TD: 43744.3   56956.6   DGPS: 41 48.618   82 51.681

Lies:	scattered	**Depth:**	20 feet
Type:	bulk freighter	**Cargo:**	coal

Power: triple expansion steam

Owner(s)   W.N. Gatfield, Sandwich, Ontario

Built: 1889 at Cleveland, Ohio by Thomas Quayle & sons

Dimensions: 286' x 42'5" x 22'   **Tonnage:**   2278 gross 1901 net

Date of Loss: Tuesday, May 1, 1917

Cause of Loss: sprung a leak and was grounded in storm

Case

Great Lakes Historical Society

Story of the Loss:

Launched July 19, 1889 as the steamer *James C. Lockwood*, she made many bulk cargo hauls on the lakes under ownership of J.D. Peterson of Huron, Ohio. In 1900 she was purchased by W.N. Gatefield of Sandwich, Ontario and renamed *Case* in honor of Mr. & Mrs. Edmond Case of the Oglebay Norton Company.

On April 30, 1917 the *Case* left Cleveland loaded with coal for Sandwich, Ontario. She sailed into a gentle breeze from the southeast and it appeared that this would be a routine crossing. As the old wooden steamer journeyed on, conditions on the lake gradually deteriorated and the wind changed from SE to SW. Within two hours, the crew of the *Case* found themselves in the midst of a full blown gale. Plowing on, the crew battled against the torrents of water cascading over her sides. Wheelsman Charles Smith found the vessel to be more and more sluggish in response to his commands. On passing Pelee Island, the vessel's flanks were exposed to the full force of the gale. Her seams opened and Captain William Allen ordered the pumps started. As the water rose it became apparent the vessel would soon sink. The captain changed course intending to ground the vessel off the lighthouse at West Sister Island, where food and shelter could be had. Even this objective became impossible, as turning the wheel required all the strength wheelsman Smith could manage. By now the water in the holds was overwhelming the pumps and the crank was splashing in the water. Again Captain Allen changed course, this time for the closer, but deserted, East Sister Island.

Slowly and sluggishly the sinking steamer responded to the efforts of her crew and turned toward the safety of East Sister Island. Smith, under the careful command of Captain Allen managed to ground the vessel on the rocks in the lea of the island, thus providing some protection from the 50 mile per hour winds that whipped the furious sea. Then additional disaster struck, fire broke out and the vessel broke apart in two places. Whipped by the strong winds, the fire rapidly engulfed the doomed ship and her crew had no choice but to take to the lifeboat. Struggling to reach shore, the crew was relieved to be greeted by George Morrison who was vacationing at a small cottage on the island. Two of the crew jumped out of the lifeboat with lines to help her land and Mr. Morrison rendered assistance. Morrison then led the men to his cottage where the fire warmed them and Mrs. Morrison served them breakfast.

Meanwhile, the lifesaving station at Marblehead had received word of the wreck and sent a motorized lifeboat on a perilous three hour journey to the wreck site. The Coast Guard boat was observed from shore but was unable to land in the heavy surf. Once again, it was Morrison to the rescue. Using the *Case's* lifeboat, he took the crew out to the Coast Guard surfboat. After the men were safely transferred to the Coast Guard boat and transported to Marblehead, Morrison resumed his vacation.

The Wreck Today:

The vessel lies scattered on a rocky bottom. Wood and metal parts can be found over a wide area.

CEI Barge

Official #:   **Site #:**   45
Location: 100 feet north of the Avon Lake, Ohio power plant breakwaters
Coordinates: TD: 43728.1 57301.2   DGPS: PA: 41 30.51   82 03.41
Lies: scattered   **Depth:**   15-20 feet
Type: barge   **Cargo:**
Power:
Owner(s)
Built:
Dimensions: **Tonnage:**
Date of Loss: mid 1920's
Cause of Loss:

Story of the Loss:

Sometime during the construction of the Avon Lake Power Plant from, 1925 to 1927, this barge was lost. The wreck site derives its name from the company that built the power plant, the Cleveland Electric Illuminating Company (CEI). Today the power plant is owned and operated by Orion Power. It is a huge landmark for boaters and aircraft.

The Wreck Today:

On the west side of the retaining wall are some very large rocks, a winch, steel cable and metal parts. Near the outflow you'll find water temperatures to be 10+ degrees warmer than prevailing water temperatures. To the north of the retaining wall, some metal chain and a tow bit are all that remain of the barge. The bottom is rock at the north side of the wall and sand closer in. There are interesting rock formations, owing in part to the plant construction.

DANGER: The east side of the plant has heavy current from the water intakes. DO NOT ENTER THE EAST SIDE. There is heavy boat and personal watercraft traffic from the boat launch to the west.

Lake Road

Miller Road
Park

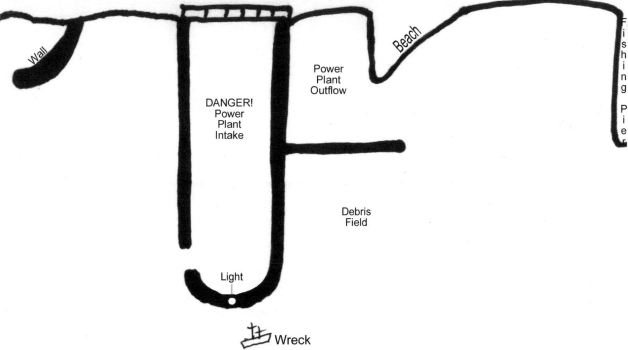

Wall

DANGER!
Power
Plant
Intake

Power
Plant
Outflow

Beach

Fishing Pier

Debris
Field

Light

Wreck

CHARGER

Official #: 5409   **Site #:** 73

Location: Pelee Passage west of Pelee Point

Coordinates: LORAN: 43812.7   57141.2   DGPS:41 51.699   82 31.800

Lies: scattered, bow south   **Depth:** 35 feet

Type: schooner   **Cargo:** wheat

Power: sail

Owner(s) Captain Lewis Bates

Built: 1868 at Sodus, New York by Diodat Rodgers

Dimensions: 136' x 25' x 10'   **Tonnage:** 277.87 gross 263.98 net

Date of Loss: Thursday, July 31, 1890

Cause of Loss: collision

Charger
Ralph Roberts' Collection

Story of the Loss:

Captain Lewis Bates and crew had left Detroit, Michigan for Buffalo, New York with 18,000 bushels of wheat. At 3:45 a.m. the steambarge *City of Cleveland* collided with the *Charger*. Crewmen John Neville and John Bell were able to escape from the damaged forecastle before the *Charger* sank, ten minutes later.

The tug *Telegram* picked up the *Charger's* crew and put them aboard the *City of Cleveland*. The crew of the *Charger* blamed the *City of Cleveland* for the accident.

From the Cleveland Plain Dealer, August 1, 1890:

Sinking of Schooner Charger Off the Dummy

Narrow Escape of the Crew

The schooner *Charger*, Capt. A.B. Bates, that left Detroit last night with 18,000 bushels of wheat for Buffalo, while abreast of the "Dummy" at 3:45 this morning was struck on her port bow by the steambarge *City of Cleveland,* which opened her up so that she sank within 10 minutes in four and one-half fathoms of water. The *City of Cleveland* sustained no damage. John Neville and John Bell were sleeping in the forecastle. The former was squeezed by broken timbers, but managed to crawl through the hole in the *Charger* and was rescued. Bell escaped through the scuttle. Capt. Bates and his crew were taken aboard the tug *Telegram* and placed upon the *City of Cleveland*, which arrived here (Cleveland, Ohio) this afternoon. There was on board the *Charger* Capt. Bates, Mate Wilson J. Pollock, Seamen John Bell, Fred Bell, John Joseph Neville, Edward Farrell, a boy named Willy Robins, and cook Sarah Cavanaugh. Neville sustained injuries and will be sent to the hospital here. The crew escaped so hastily that they saved nothing. It was blowing very fresh at the time and the *City of Cleveland* was flying light. Capt. Christie Moran of the *City of Cleveland* was not disposed to talk about the accident. He and his crew spent part of the afternoon in the office of a leading law firm here. Some of the crew of the *Charger* think the steambarge, on account of being light in a heavy sea, did not steer well.

For some time after the sinking, the *Charger* posed a serious hazard to navigation in the narrow Pelee Passage. The Sunday, August 17, 1890 *Cleveland Plain Dealer* ran an article on the dangers the masts posed to passing vessels. According to the article, it was reported "at least twenty-five boats were bunched together and were unable to make much headway until daylight" because of this obstruction.

The Wreck Today:

The *Charger* is located on a silt bottom just west of the *David Vance*. Among Canadian divers, this site is called the "*Capstan*" wreck. The wreck has a capstan (of course) and also a wheel, windlass, and dead-eyes. The *Vance* (known to Canadians as the *Wheel Wreck*) lies in the same location, so if you come across a second wheel to the east, you've found the *David Vance*.

CITY OF CONCORD

Official #:	5538	**Site #:**	69
Location:	10 miles north of Huron, Ohio		
Coordinates:	LORAN: 43675.0 57052.7	DGPS: 41 32.728 82 32.811	
Lies:	bow east	**Depth:**	45 feet
Type:	wood steamer	**Cargo:**	coal
Power:	steam, 26" diameter cylinder: 36" stroke		
Owner(s)	Norman Mills		
Built:	1868 at Cleveland, Ohio by Lafrinnier & Drake		
Dimensions:	135'2" x 25'8" x 11'	**Tonnage:**	
Date of Loss:	Saturday, September 29, 1906		
Cause of Loss:	storm		

City of Concord
Historical Collections of the Great Lakes

Story of the Loss:

Launched on July 16, 1868, this oak hulled vessel was touted as "a model of her class in all respects ... with such improvements as experience suggests (*Toledo Blade*, July 18, 1868) ." She was originally built as a package freighter/passenger vessel. She was converted to a lumber carrier in 1890. She nearly sank in August of 1906 when her consorts tow line fowled in the propeller. She survived this event only to sink under far worse circumstances a month later.

With consorts, *Montpelier* and *Donaldson* in tow, The *City of Concord* left Cleveland Harbor for St. Clair, Michigan the morning of September 29, 1890. She stopped in Lorain to pick up a third consort, *Neguanee*, and was on her way again by 4:00 p.m. Only a few hours had passed when the remnants of a gulf hurricane caught up to them off Huron, Ohio. Making little headway against the gale, the *Concord* began to take on water about 8:30 p.m. The pumps could not keep up and *Concord* cast off her consorts.

When the rising water reached the boilers, all hope was lost and Captain Charles McEcheran ordered the crew to abandon ship. Two of the crew refused to board the yawl boat and died with the *City of Concord*. A third crewman, Roy Wakefield, leapt for the yawl as it cleared the sinking vessel. He missed and was not seen again by those in the yawl. Believing Wakefield to be lost and seeing the *Concord* sink, the yawl made for the nearest consort, *Monpelier*. However, the *Monpelier* was in imminent danger of sinking and the 9 people in the yawl had to make for shore.

Fighting monstrous waves the yawl boat survived a fifteen mile voyage and dumped the near dead crew on shore about 2 miles east of Cedar Point. Fortunately for young Roy Wakefield, the barge *Donaldson* was able to pick him up and take him to safety at Huron.

The *Monpelier* and *Donaldson* made it to safety. The *Neguanee,* driven ashore near where the yawl boat landed, was a total loss but her crew survived.

The Wreck Today:

The *City of Concord* lies upright in 45 feet of water. The center of the vessel is broken up but some decking remains at the stern. It is possible to get between decks without knowing it if you are not careful. Look for her rudder, prop, large double-boiler, capstan, and windlass.

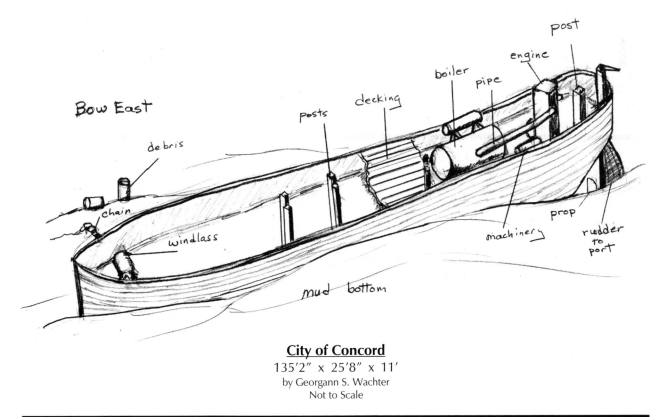

City of Concord
135'2" x 25'8" x 11'
by Georgann S. Wachter
Not to Scale

CIVIL WAR WRECK

Official #:   **Site #:**   54

Location: 20 miles north of Lorain, Ohio

Coordinates: LORAN: 43817.5   57274.3   DGPS: 41 46.068   82 13.747

Lies: bow northeast   **Depth:**   65 feet

Type: two masted sail   **Cargo:**   stone

Power: sail

Owner(s)

Built: early 1800's

Dimensions: approximately 72' long x 16' wide **Tonnage:**

Date of Loss: probably 1860's

Cause of Loss   appears to have burned

Shoe and Spike on the "Civil War" Wreck
Phyllis Ruetschle

Story of the Loss:

Visual inspection of the wreck indicates there was a fire onboard when she was lost.

The Wreck Today:

This small vessel appears to have foundered in the 1860's. She presents a very low profile. The stern is square. What was a small cabin is now gone, as is most of her decking. Tiller steered, there are no deadeyes but blocks were used on her masts. The vessel has a slight list to port and one of her masts has fallen to her port side.

Divers should watch out for the gill nets snagged on this wreck.

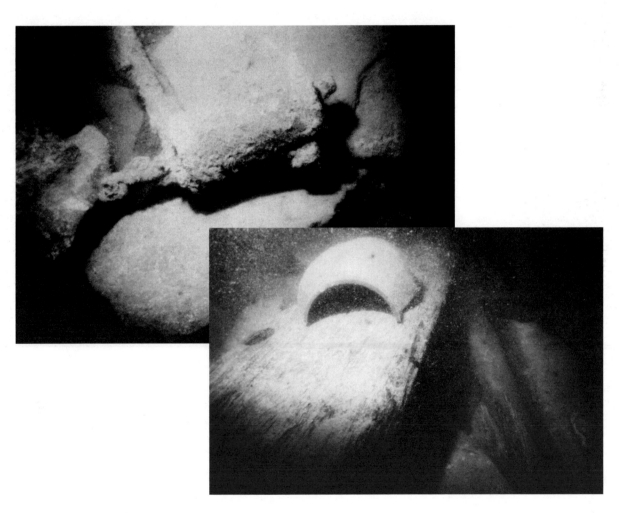

*Metal objects and pot shards were among the artifacts discovered on the "Civil War" wreck.
Photos by Phyllis Ruetschle.*

CLARION

Official #:	125937	**Site #:**	58

Location: In Canadian waters 30 miles north of Lorain, Ohio and approximately 13miles north east of Point Pelee

Coordinates: LORAN: 43890.1 57297.7   DGPS: 41 57.263   82 16.311

Lies: bow southwest   **Depth:** 75 feet

Type: composite propeller   **Cargo:** flour, corn, mixed cargo

Power: Compound, 27" diameter cylinder 44" x 40" stroke built 1881 by Dry Dock Engine Works Detroit, Michigan, one 12' x 14'6" scotch boiler

Owner(s) Anchor Line Company, Buffalo, New York

Built: 1881 at Wyandotte, Michigan by Detroit Dry Dock Company. Hull #45

Dimensions: 240'9" x 36'1" x 15'5"   **Tonnage:** 1711 gross 1573.33 net

Date of Loss: Thursday, December 8, 1909

Cause of Loss: Fire / storm

Clarion
Great Lakes Historical Society

Story of the Loss:

Launched July 27, 1881. The *Clarion* served for 28 years as a package freighter hauling for the Pennsylvania Railroad. From Buffalo to Chicago to Duluth, she called on all the U.S. cities on the Great Lakes. As a "line boat", she carried anything that could be put in a railroad box car. Painted green from the water line to the main deck, her hull was white above the main deck. Her stacks were bright red and she carried one tall yellow mast aft of the pilot house.

With plans to lay up in Erie for the winter, the *Clarion* was making her last trip of the season. Bound from Chicago to Buffalo, she was purported to be carrying two locomotives. The voyage had been unremarkable as she and the freighter *Denmark* steamed down river past Detroit at 1:45 p.m.

Thirty miles further east, as the ship passed the *Kewaunee* lightship at Southeast Shoal, the *Clarion* was encountering angry water and swirling snow. At 7:00 p.m., only a mile and a half from the lightship, fire broke out in the hold. Mate James Thompson entered the hold with a fire extinguisher and was never seen again. As the crew attempted to battle the rapidly spreading fire with the steam fire extinguisher, the ship began to drift with the storm. The blazing fire separated the crew. Captain Thomas Bell and 12 crewmen trapped forward took to the lifeboat and were lost at sea attempting to reach the lightship *Kewaunee*. Chief Engineer A.E. Welch and five crewmen trapped aft lost the small wooden lifeboat while attempting to launch it. In a valiant effort to retrieve the lifeboat, oiler George Macaulay was swept to sea by a monstrous wave.

As other ships passed without rendering assistance, the steamer *Josiah C. Munro* grounded on Southeast Shoal attempting a rescue. Huddled on the stern with little hope of living, the six surviving crewmen sighted the lights of the *L.C. Hanna*. Under command of Captain Mathew Anderson, the the *L.C. Hanna* made two unsuccessful attempts to bring her bow against the stern of the dying ship. Thwarted by heavy seas on his first two efforts, Anderson brought his bow under the stern of the *Clarion* permitting six survivors to leap to the safety of the *Hanna*. The rescue was so notable that a Leonard Haunah wrote a poem about it.

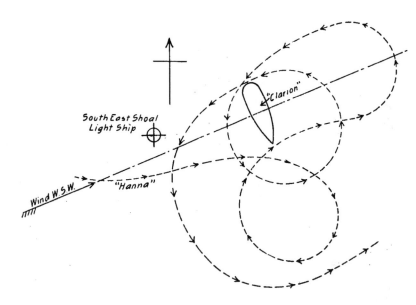

Diagram showing Hanna's maneuvers. Reproduced from The Marine Review, January 1910.

Crewmen from the lightboat told of the burning *Clarion* passing within 100 feet of the lightboat and then seeing her sink about 200 feet away. (Authors note: she actually sank many miles to the east.) Their attempts to launch a lifeboat were thwarted by icy waves bounding over the decks of the tiny *Kewaunee*.

George Macaulay's body was recovered in the spring and is buried in Southampton, Ontario.

Lost in the same storm, were the *W. C. Richardson* near Buffalo, and the car ferry *Marquette & Bessemer No.2* between Port Stanley and Erieau, Ontario.

The Wreck Today:

With the stern section amazingly intact, the *Clarion* lies upright in 75 feet of water. The bow is so badly distorted by the fire that the first divers to find her believed she had no bow. Not knowing what wreck they had found, they called the wreck the "Stern Section". You will find locomotive wheels in the hold. A large hemp fishnet hangs over the starboard side of the bow section and additional net is snagged at the rudder. Moving forward from the tiller, divers will find bollards, a capstan, the engine, stack hole, and a large hatch before arriving at the break in her mid section.

CLEVECO

Official #:	211035	**Site #:**	10
Location:	14 miles north of Euclid, Ohio		
Coordinates:	LORAN: 43926.2 57609.5	DGPS: 41 47.473 81 36.000	
Lies:	turtled, north - south	**Depth:**	77 feet
Type:	tanker barge	**Cargo:**	1 million gallons fuel oil
Power:	towed		
Owner(s)	Cleveland Tankers, Inc.		
Built:	1913 by American Shipbuilding Co., Lorain, Ohio. Hull #702		
Dimensions:	260' x 43' x 25'1"	**Tonnage:**	2441 gross
Date of Loss:	Wednesday, December 2, 1942		
Cause of Loss:	Swamped in storm after her tow, the tug *Admiral*, foundered		

Cleveco
Great Lakes Historical Society

Story of the Loss:

Built for the Standard Oil Company, the *Cleveco* was originally named *S.O. Co. #85*. Renamed *S.T. Co. #85* in 1916, *Socony #85* in 1921, and *Gotham* in 1929. She was dubbed *Cleveco* in 1940.

The *Cleveco* left Toledo at 2:45 p.m. Tuesday, December 1, 1942 in tow of the tug *Admiral*. She carried a crew of 18 and one million gallons of fuel oil. About 4:00 a.m. December 2, the vessels encountered a severe storm. By 6:30 a.m. the winds were 70 miles per hour and the waves were running 18 feet. *Cleveco's* Captain, William H. Smith, radioed for help when watchmen on the barge could not see the *Admiral's* lights and noticed the tow line to the *Admiral* had dropped into the water. Apparently the tug had sunk in the stormy darkness, taking the lives of 14 seamen.

Captain Smith gave his position as about 15 miles off Avon Point. He indicated the *Cleveco* was in no immediate danger. However, the storm was getting worse. Two tugs were dispatched to the powerless barge. At some point the towline joining the *Cleveco* to the *Admiral* was either broken or (more likely) cut.

Adrift in the dark, stormy night, the *Cleveco's* position was uncertain. Civil Air Patrol pilot, Clara Livingston, spotted the barge 10 miles north of Cleveland and the Coast Guard cutter *Ossipee* changed course to intercept her. The *Ossipee* spotted the *Cleveco* briefly. However the 70 mile per hour winds, driving snow, and mist made sighting the hapless vessel difficult.

Captain Smith maintained radio contact with the rescue vessels throughout the afternoon of December 2. Smith indicated the situation was rapidly deteriorating. Water was rising in the holds and would soon put out the generators powering his radio. In his last message at 4:30 p.m., Smith feared for his vessels safety.

The *Ossipee* searched vainly through the night. In the morning, her ice coated crew found two bodies wearing *Cleveco* life jackets. In total, 18 men were lost on the *Cleveco*. Of her crew, only Captain Smith's body was not recovered.

Cleveco being raised by the work barge Rebel. Photo from the Remickk Collection

The Wreck Today:

In 1961, salvors raised the barge to remove it as a hazard to navigation and recover the industrial fuel oil. When storms again threatened, the fuel oil recovery was cut short and the barge was sunk in deeper water off Euclid, Ohio.

Fuel oil was discovered to be leaking from the barge in 1994, and in 1995 approximately 500,000 gallons of oil were removed and the tanks sealed. The vessel lies upside down with her superstructure crushed in the mud. She rises about 14 feet off the bottom. Six sealed valves, remnants of the first salvage attempt, run along her keel.

H. G. Cleveland

Official #:	11762	**Site #:**	32
Location:	4 miles off Lakewood, Ohio		
Coordinates:	LORAN: 43775.5 57436.1	DGPS: 41 32.050 81 48.611	
Lies:	bow east	**Depth:**	55 feet
Type:	schooner	**Cargo:**	Stone
Power:	sail		
Owner(s)	Captain Frank Jennings		
Built:	1867 on the Black River at Lorain, Ohio by William Jones		
Dimensions:	137'2" x 25'8" x 10'4"	**Tonnage:**	264 gross
Date of Loss:	Monday, August 14, 1899		
Cause of Loss:	foundered		

H. G. Cleveland

Remickk Collection

Story of the Loss:

The *H.G. Cleveland* left Kelleys Island about 9:00 the evening of Saturday, August 12 and headed for Cleveland with a load of quarry stone. It was between 11:00 p.m. and midnight that the crew discovered a leak in the vessel. As the water was pouring in, all hands were ordered below to the pumps, and they worked for their very lives all through the night and into the early hours of the morning.

Approaching Cleveland, the *City of Detroit* sighted a solitary crewman on the deck of the *H.G. Cleveland* waving a torch as a signal of distress. As the *City of Detroit* hove to and circled to render assistance, the lone figure aboard the *Cleveland* disappeared below decks. Sighting the name on the bow of the distressed vessel, Captain McKay of the Detroit hailed "*Cleveland* Ahoy!" Shortly thereafter a crewman appeared and cried out, "Aye, aye sir. All hands at the pumps, sir. The schooner's leaking and the water's gaining on the pumps sir. Throw us a line." Realizing that the vessel was too far gone to be towed to shore, Captain McKay offered to take the crew of the *H.G. Cleveland* aboard the *City of Detroit*. Undaunted they declined the offer, declaring they would stay at the pumps as long as their vessel had two planks together!

McKay then brought the great steamship abreast of the stricken schooner and lowered his lifeboat and two crewmen to provide assistance to the schooner's crew when she finally when down. He then pulled away and headed for Cleveland to give notice to the life saving station. En route, they met the V.O.T. tug *Thomas Matham* with the lifesavers aboard on their way to the schooner.

On arriving at the *H.G. Cleveland*, the *Matham* was made fast to the schooner and began to tow her toward the port of Cleveland. At the same time all of the lifesavers, the crew of the *Matham*, and the two crewmembers from the *City of Detroit* took to working the pumps. The crew of the *H.G. Cleveland* was completely exhausted from their long ordeal and welcomed being relieved at the pumps. The struggle against the relentless flow of water continued for the next six hours as the *Matham* towed the *Cleveland* six miles closer to Cleveland. Then, with the spires of the city in sight, ominous creaking and groaning from the bowels of the schooner signaled her final demise. Hastily, the men scrambled aboard the tug *Matham*. Just as the last leapt to the tug, the schooner succumbed and settled to the bottom.

The Wreck Today:

Don't be fooled into thinking you are diving one of Lake Erie's famous rock piles. The hull of the *Cleveland* has split open under the weight of her stone cargo. She lays in the mud with her center board protruding through her cargo and planks scattered about her. Obvious features of the wreck are the windlass, some anchor chain, and cable.

JAMES B. COLGATE

Official #: 77019   **Site #:** 11

Location: 8 miles southwest of Erieau, Ontario Canada

Coordinates: LORAN: 44032.5 57607.7   DGPS: 42 05.376   81 44.279

Lies: bow northeast   **Depth:**

Type: whaleback steamer   **Cargo:** coal

Power: 1000 HP triple expansion engine from Marquette Iron Works, Duluth, Minnesota

Owner(s) Standard Transit Company, Cleveland, Ohio 1915-16; Pittsburgh Steamship Company, Cleveland, Ohio, 1901-15; Bessemer Steamship Company, Duluth, Minnesota, 1900-01; American Steel Barge Company, Duluth, Minnesota 1892-1900

Built: 1892 at Superior, Wisconsin by American Steel Barge Company Hull #121

Dimensions: 308' x 38' x 24'   **Tonnage:** 1713 gross   1318 net

Date of Loss: Black Friday, October 20, 1916

Cause of Loss: storm

James B. Colgate
Great Lakes Historical Society

Story of the Loss:

The *Colgate* was launched on September 21, 1892.

Early on October 20, 1916, The *Colgate* left Buffalo and sailed into the teeth of what would come to be called the "Black Friday Storm." About 2 p.m., the wind shifted to the southwest and brought a sudden squall. Newly appointed Captain, former 1st mate Walter Grashaw stood at the helm, confident in his boat and his 14 years experience sailing the Great Lakes. He commented to his crew, "It's a ripsnorter all right, but we'll pull through." Shortly after 4 o'clock in the afternoon, the wind was hitting peaks of 75 mph. Captain Grashaw tried to head the "pig boat" into the gale. According to the captain, "About 4 bells all was well. Then, suddenly, the storm hit. The boat started to list. It jerked with a heavy motion." Grashaw said, "It would have been murder to order a man forward to find what the trouble was." (*Plain Dealer*, October 24, 1916) By 10 p.m. it was apparent she would soon go down. The captain attempted to order his crew to the lifeboats but he could not be heard over of the incredible force of the screeching winds that would soon sink the *Colgate*.

As a terrible shudder raked the boat, she nosed down and plunged head first beneath the waves. Captain Grashaw, Engineer Harry Ossman, and an unnamed oiler grabbed onto a raft as 19 others perished instantly. Three hours later, a wave flipped the raft and swept the oiler to his death. After drifting all day Saturday, another cold wave of water overturned the raft and Engineer Harry Ossman never returned. In the captains own words:

"Death stayed there with me on that raft every minute. I knew it was there waiting. There was no line on the raft to hang onto. Four hours after the Colgate went down, a

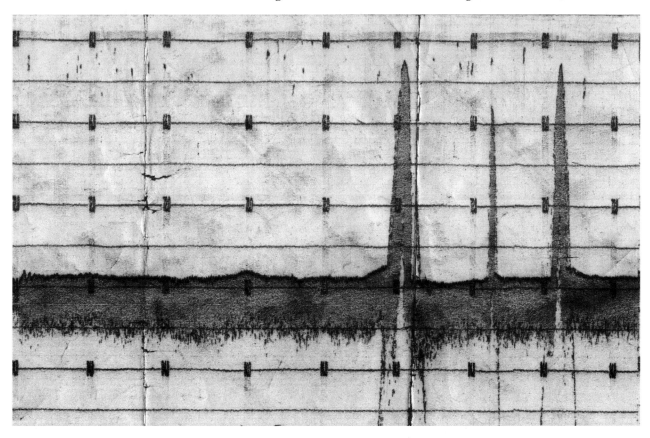

Sonar image of the James B. Colgate

big wave flipped our raft over and the oiler was carried away. We drifted all day Saturday. Our hands were numb. We took turns standing up and sitting down to keep our blood in circulation. It began to get rougher toward night. Our raft capsized twice, and it was all we could do to climb back on again.

I tried to cheer my mate by telling him we would soon be picked up. But I was talking with my mouth, not my heart. About 11:00 p.m. our raft flipped over again. The engineer was so weak he could not get back on. All night I seemed to see two men floating around me. It almost drove me mad.

At 7:00 a.m. Sunday, the steamer City of Detroit, headed from Buffalo to Detroit, passed. I waved my arms but the lookout didn't see me. Suddenly, there were 10 short blasts back of me. I jumped to my feet again and nearly fell into the water. About a quarter of a mile away was a ferry — the finest sight I ever saw. I yelled like a madman."

Captain Grashaw, sole survivor of the tragedy, was rescued Sunday morning by the replacement *Marquette & Bessemer #2* after 35 hours in the raft.

The Black Friday storm was driven by two converging high pressure systems and the remnants of an

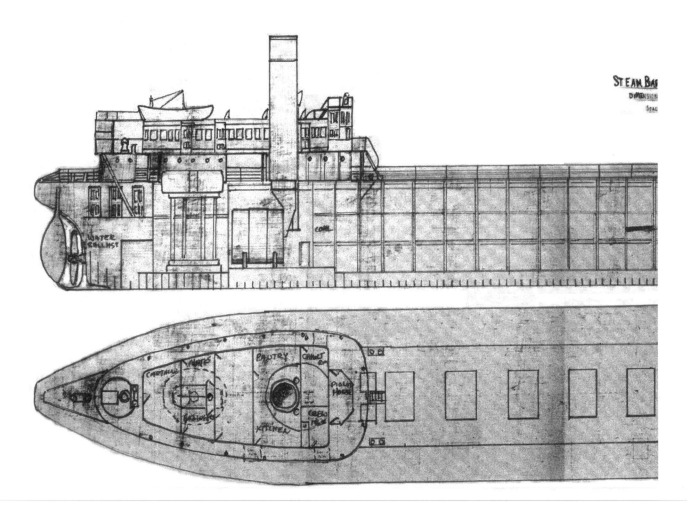

Stern section blueprint for the James B. Colgate

unnamed hurricane that came up from the Gulf Coast. It is the worst storm ever recorded on Lake Erie. Also lost in this awful storm were the *Merida* with no survivors, the *Marshall F. Butters*, and the *D.L. Filer* and six of her crew.

The Wreck Today:

The *James B. Colgate* lies upside down with more of her starboard side protruding from the mud bottom. Her prop makes a nice setting for photos. Much of her superstructure, a stack, air scoop, and other debris lay in the sizable debris field just north of the stern.

CAUTION: this site is subject to occasional strong currents on both the surface and at depth.

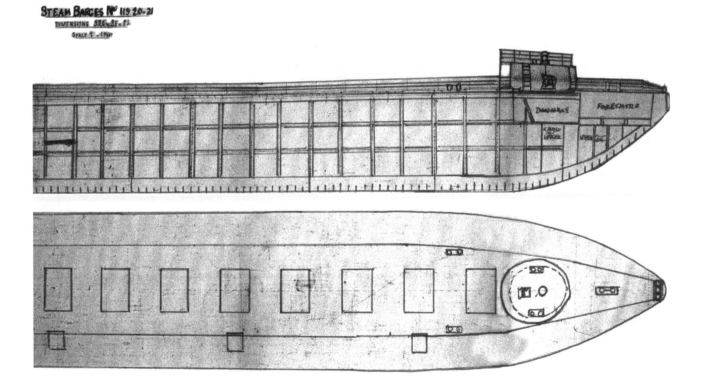

Bow section blueprint for the James B. Colgate

COLONEL COOK

Official #: 4366   **Site #:** 44

Location: ¼ mile offshore of Avon Lake, Ohio

Coordinates: APPROXIMATE: LORAN: 43730.5 57308.2 DGPS: 41 30.540 82 02.527

Lies: scattered   **Depth:** 10-20 feet

Type: schooner / barge   **Cargo:** stone

Power: sail

Owner(s) L.P. and J.A. Smith of Cleveland, Ohio

Built: 1855 at Oswego, New York by James Navagh

Dimensions: 128'9" x 25'4" x 11'2"   **Tonnage:** 266 gross 252 net

Date of Loss: Sunday, September 23, 1894

Cause of Loss: sprung a leak

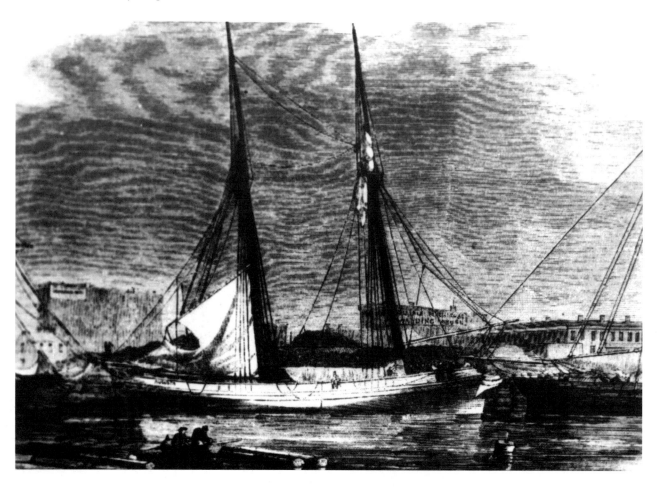

Colonel Cook as Augusta

at dock in Chicago after colliding with the Lady Elgin from Frank Leslies Illustrated Newspaper
Historical Collections of the Great Lakes

Her Sordid Past:

The schooner *Colonel Cook* lives in infamy. As the *Augusta* she was responsible for the second worst maritime disaster in the history of the Great Lakes. On the 7th of September in 1860, the 252 foot paddle wheeler, *Lady Elgin* left Chicago on a return voyage to Milwaukee. She carried approximately 300 military Union Guards on an excursion, about 50 other passengers, and 45 crew. At 2:00 a.m. on September 8th, out of the blackness came the schooner *Augusta*, crashing into the *Lady Elgin* aft of the wheel on the port side. *Lady Elgin* sank so quickly that only 18 of the passengers survived. Almost 300 people lost their lives in the cold waters of Lake Michigan in the dark of the night. It is unclear whether the *Augusta* even offered to help the steamer.

From the *Detroit Free Press*, September 9, 1860:

TERRIBLE DISASTER.

The Steamer Lady Elgin
Sunk, by Collision, in Lake Michigan

OVER THREE HUNDRED LIVES LOST.
Statement of the Clerk

Letter to Superintendent Rice of the Michigan Central Railroad

The steamer Lady Elgin, of the Lake Superior Line, which left here last night, was run into by the schooner Augusta, off Waukegan, at half past 2 this morning, striking her abaft the wheel. The steamer sunk in twenty minutes in three hundred feet of water. Only seventeen persons are known to be saved, including the clerk, steward, and porter. From three hundred fifty to four hundred persons are said to have been aboard, among them were the Black Yagers, Green Yagers, and Rifles, and several fire companies from Milwaukee, who were on a visit to this city. Col. Lumsden of the New Orleans *Picayune*, and his family were also on board and are supposed to be lost. At the time of the accident, the schooner was sailing at the rate of eleven miles per hour. The steam tug McQueen left this morning for the scene of the disaster. Further particulars will be given on her return. The names of those saved, as far as known, are as follows: … The books and papers are all lost. After the collision, the steamer floated south to Winetka, where she sank.

The clerk makes the following statement: The Lady Elgin left the port of Chicago at half past 11 o'clock for Lake Superior. Among her passengers were the Union Guards, of Milwaukee, composing part of some 150 excursionists from that city. About half past 2 o'clock this morning the schooner Augusta, of Oswego, came in collision with the Lady Elgin when about ten miles from shore. The vessel struck the steamer at the midships gangway on the larboard side. The two separated instantly and the Augusta drifted by in the darkness. At the moment of the collision, there was music and dancing forward in the cabin. In an instant after the crash, it was still, and in half an hour the steamer sank. I passed through the cabins. The ladies were pale but silent. There was not a cry nor shriek; no sound but the rush of steam and the surge of the heavy seas. Whether they were not fully aware of the danger, or whether their appalling situation made them speechless, I cannot tell. Boats were lowered at once, with the design of going round on the larboard side to examine the leak. There were two oars, but just at the moment, some person possessed himself of one of them, and we were left powerless to manage the boat. We succeeded once in reaching the wheel but were lifted away and thrown upon the beach at Winetka. Only two boats left the steamer. One of them contained thirteen persons, all of whom were saved. The other bore eight; but four reached the shore alive, the others being drowned at the beach. Before I left the steamer, the engine had ceased work, the fires having been extinguished, and within thirty minutes, the Lady Elgin disappeared. The force and direction of the wind were such that the boats and fragments were driven up the lake and would reach shore in the vicinity of Winetka. As I stood upon the beach, helplessly looking back along the route we had drifted, I could see in the gray of the morning objects floating upon the water, and sometimes I thought human beings struggling with the waters.

(signed) H.G. Caryl, Clerk of the Lady Elgin

Upon reaching Chicago, Captain D.M. Malott reported that his damaged schooner had hit a steamer near Waukegan. The *Augusta* was not welcome in Milwaukee, which most of the victims called home. In fact, a mob planned to burn the ship. Within a year, in an effort to hide her reputation, the *Augusta* was painted black and renamed the *Colonel Cook*. Four years later, Captain Nelse Malott and other former crewmen of the *Augusta*, now crewing the *Mojave*, disappeared without a trace on Lake Michigan.

Lady Elgin
Remick Collection

Story of the Loss:

The jinxed *Colonel Cook* became a salt water vessel, traveling to New York City, Mobile, Alabama, Cuba, and Texas ports before returning to the Great Lakes where she sank near Sandusky in 1891. She was raised and sank again inside the Cleveland breakwall in 1892. She was raised once again, only to meet her final fate two years later.

On September 23, 1894, the *Colonel Cook* and the *Walton* were in tow of the tug *J.R. Sprankle* bound from Kelleys Island to Cleveland. Off Avon Point, the *Cook* sprung a leak and her captain drew close to the *Walton* so her crew could help bail. However, as befits her reputation, the *Cook's* crew jumped ship as soon as they were close enough to the *Walton* to get aboard her. The captain followed suit and cut the tow line allowing the *Colonel Cook* to drift into shore where she broke up in 11 feet of water.

The Wreck Today:

Scattered remains of a schooner have been located on a rock bottom one quarter mile out, east of the Avon Lake power plant. A sixteen foot high rudder near shore disappeared over the winter of 1998/ 1999. These are believed to be vestiges of the *Colonel Cook*.

Tug J.R. Sprankle
Remick Collection

COLONIAL

Official #:	126012	**Site #:**	17

Location: 7 miles west of Erieau, Ontario, ¼ mile offshore

Coordinates: LORAN: 44042.5 57472.5   DGPS: 42 15 062   82 04 289

Lies: bow southwest (230°)   **Depth:**   20 feet

Type: wood propeller   **Cargo:**   hard coal

Power: 725 HP fore and aft compound engine

Owner(s)   Reed Wrecking Company, Sarnia, Ontario

Built: 1882 at Cleveland, Ohio by George Presley & Company

Dimensions: 244'5" x 36'3" x 19'2"   **Tonnage:**   1713 gross   1323 net

Date of Loss: Friday, November 13, 1914

Cause of Loss: foundered

Colonial

Great Lakes Historical Society

Story of the Loss:

Launched March 18, 1882, the *Colonial* was converted to a bulk freighter in 1899 at the Globe Iron Works, Cleveland, Ohio. She was rebuilt in November 1914. Original dimensions were 244'5" x 36'3" x 22'9", 1501 gross tons, 1188 net tons.

Having sailed from Oswego, New York via the Welland Canal, The *Colonial* entered Lake Erie laden with 2,000 pounds of hard coal on November 12, 1914. Once on the lake, she encountered a southwest gale with 70 mile per hour winds and heavy seas. While pounding through the storm, the *Colonial* sprang a leak and the engine crew was ordered to the pumps. Shortly after passing Rondeau Harbor, the water rising in the hold forced the crew topsides and Captain J. E. Cooper headed his sinking vessel toward the Canadian shore, back to Rondeau Harbor.

Blown closer to shore than Captain Cooper planned, the vessel was on the verge of sinking when she ran aground a quarter mile off the beach. All fifteen men aboard took to the lifeboat and, guided by the lights of the church that still marks the spot where she lays, rowed to the safety of shore. En route to shore the lifeboat capsized once but was righted. The crew was sheltered and warmed in the Pardo family home which still stands nearby.

The Wreck Today:

Remarkably intact for a shallow water site, the *Colonial* lays on a hard bottom scattered over a wide area. In addition to the boiler and engine, look carefully for a variety of items; including, brass gauges, sinks, chain, cable, windlass, portholes, kitchenware, and blocks. Kent Divers Association of Chatham, Ontario has mounted the bell in concrete and placed it amidships west of the boiler.

Conemaugh

Official #:	125858	**Site #:**	75
Location:	west side of Pelee Point		
Coordinates:	LORAN: 43835.7 57163.1	DGPS 41 54.570 82.30.655	
Lies:	scattered, bow northwest	**Depth:**	20 feet
Type:	Wood freighter with hogging braces	**Cargo:**	package freight
Power:	steam propeller, steeple compound engine		
Owner(s)	Erie & Western Transit Company, Buffalo, New York		
Built:	1880 at North Bay City, Michigan by F.W. Wheeler and Frederick Jones		
Dimensions:	251' x 36 ' 15'3"	**Tonnage:**	1609.53 gross 1453.11 net
Date of Loss:	Wednesday, November 21, 1906		
Cause of Loss:	storm		

Conemaugh
Great Lakes Historical Society

Story of the Loss:

Bound from Fairport, Ohio to Chicago, the *Conemaugh* encountered a fierce gale. The 251 foot wood steamer was driven ashore on Point Pelee. Stranded on the beach, she was pounded on the rocks by the wind driven sea. As she filled with water, her crew of 22 was rescued by the lifesavers from the Point Pelee Life Saving Station. All hope of recovering the vessel was abandoned as the waves continued their relentless attack on the grounded vessel. First her port deck was cracked and then a hole opened in the main deck. Her sternpost was driven three feet forward by strong surges in the 9 foot deep water.

Small solace can be taken in the fact that the *Conemaugh* was not alone in her troubles in this blustery gale. The *Duluth Evening Herald* reported twelve vessels and seventeen lives were lost on the Great Lakes. Other news services reported 23 lives lost. The barge *Resolute* sank off Toronto, killing six men. The barge *Athens* was lost off Sandusky Ohio, killing seven men. Four men died in another incident at Muskegon, Michigan. Several other vessels on Lake Erie were damaged and the steamer *Charles B. Hill* ran aground and was lost off Madison, Ohio.

During a six day period, the lighter *T.F. Newman* was able to put in 22 hours at the *Conemaugh* wreck site. She salvaged much of her $50,000 cargo of dry goods but the ship became a total loss before she could be pulled off. Among the cargo salvaged were 130 bags of oyster shells, 1000 packages of canned goods, and 799 cases of dry goods.

The Wreck Today:

She is located on a sand bottom and much of the wreck is covered by sand. This site could be a shore dive from Point Pelee National Park. A shore plaque in the park marks the area. The prop is broken and there is a boiler with lots of carp.

The largest portion of wreckage is located 35 feet from the stern. At the stern you can find her four propeller blades buried in the sand. The blades were apparently broken off when the vessel was driven aground.

Watch for boat traffic.

CORTLAND

Official #: 5397 **Site #:** 52

Location: 21 miles north-northeast of Vermilion, Ohio 28 miles from Cleveland, Ohio on a line to Pelee Point.

Coordinates: sorry, still secret

Lies: bow northeast **Depth:** 70 feet

Type: bark **Cargo:** iron ore

Power: 3 masted sail

Owner(s) A.P. Lyman of Sheboygan, Wisconsin

Built: 1867 at Sheboygan, Wisconsin by Albin G. Huntley

Dimensions: 173'6" x 34'4" x 13'8" **Tonnage:** 676 gross

Date of Loss: Saturday, June 20, 1868

Cause of Loss: collision

Cortland
Historical Collections of the Great Lakes

Story of the Loss:

The *Cortland* had left Sheboygan laden with iron ore. On board were Captain Lawton, 13 crew and a young male passenger named Billy. Stories have it that young Billy, the nephew of Captain Lawton, was a sickly child and was sent to sea for his health. Her passage downbound to the Iron Mountain Mining Company of Cleveland took her through the narrow northern passage and past Point Pelee. As the vessel crossed Lake Erie June 20,1868, the night was dark and a gentle breeze lapped waves against the side of the bark rigged *Cortland*. Midnight approached and the crew had every reason to believe this would be an uneventful passage. Unfortunately, a bizarre series of events was about to unfold.

Crewman Andrew Brown reported to the first mate that they were approaching a large steamer. Mr. Brown also noted that the green light on the bark was dim. The first mate took the oil light down to trim it — leaving no green light in the rigging. Unable to see the bark, the approaching steamer continued on a collision course toward the *Cortland*. For the next twenty minutes, Brown watched as the oncoming steamer marched inexorably on toward the *Cortland*. Seeing the imminent collision, crewman Brown began furiously ringing the ship's bell. The first mate emerged from below decks with a now brightly burning green light. However, as he was replacing the light, the sidewheel steamer *Morning Star* collided with the *Cortland*. The collision killed the first mate instantly.

One other crewmen on the *Cortland* was killed as the *Morning Star,* rammed the *Cortland* near the stern on her starboard side. One of the sailors, Mr. Tripp, had been put in charge of young Billy. Tripp carried Billy to the foremast and, to prevent him from being washed to sea, lashed him to the upper yard arms. The sidewheels of the *Morning Star* continued to turn, tearing gaping holes in the *Cortland*. As she settled, the foremast snapped and, Billy tumbled to the water. Tripp hurried to rescue the young boy, cutting him free with his knife. The two now struggled in the midst of the mayhem occurring around them to reach the safety of the mainmast.

Both Captain Viger of the *Morning Star* and Captain Lawton of the *Cortland* realized their vessels were doomed and sought to save their respective crews. Two injured crewmen and nine others escaped the *Cortland*, some clinging to the cabin structure as it broke from the vessel and floated free. Approximately 36 people lost their lives on the *Morning Star*.

This incident led to a change in the rules for lighting sailing vessels.

The Wreck Today:

The *Cortland* has been located but information on its location is still closely held. She sits with about a 30 degree list to starboard and the damage done to her by the sidewheel of the *Morning Star* is evident.

Collision of the Cortland & Morning Star
Painting by Diane Boldman, Avon Lake, Ohio

CRAFTSMAN

Official #: 221068

Location: 1 mile north of Avon Lake, Ohio

Coordinates: LORAN: 43745.6 57332.6

Site #: 40

DGPS: Barge: 41 31.942   82 00.375

Crain: 41 31.932   82 00.355

Lies: bow west, crane is east of barge

Type: derrick barge

Power: towed

Owner(s) L. A. Wells Construction Co., Cleveland

Built: 1921 at Lorain, Ohio by American Ship Building Company

Dimensions: 90′ 1″ x 28′1″ x 8′ 3″

Date of Loss: Tuesday, June 3, 1958

Cause of Loss: foundered

Depth: 41 feet

Cargo: steam powered derrick

Tonnage: 165 gross

Craftsman
Historical Collections of the Great Lakes

Story of the Loss:

Her original dimensions were 83′6″ x 28′1″ x 8′ 2″ & 163 gross tons. She was rebuilt in 1946.

The *Craftsman* had recently completed work on a gas line being laid under the Huron River at Huron, Ohio. She was being towed back to Cleveland by the tug *Toledo* and was just off of Avon Point when the 90 foot barge began to founder. The two crewmen aboard struggled for an hour to keep the barge afloat.

The *Toledo* radioed for help about 7 p.m. Coast Guard Station Lorain responded and called station Cleveland for additional assistance as their 40 foot patrol boat headed out into 5 to 6 foot waves and 20-25 mph winds. Coast Guard Station Cleveland dispatched the cutter *Kaw* and a 40 foot escort vessel to the scene. As Coastguardsmen approached the *Craftsman*, they observed her roll on her side and then turn over. Two crewmen, John Hendrickson and Lester Young, were pitched into the water as the barge capsized. They fought to stay afloat as a strong current

Young & Hendrickson in ambulance after their rescue by the Coast Guard. Cleveland Plain Dealer, June 4, 1958.

tried to pull them under. Life buoys were thrown to them by the onrushing Coast Guard patrol boat from Lorain. According to Hendrickson, "We'd have gone down if the Coast Guard hadn't thrown that life preserver to us. I could feel the pull of the water as the scow went down when I reached for the buoy. The Coast Guard made a very nice pickup."

Both crewmen were treated for exposure at Saint Joseph's Hospital, Lorain, Ohio.

The Wreck Today:

The barge lays upright on a hard bottom with the bow pointing west. There are a couple winches on deck and hatches leading into a mud filled interior. More than one diver has been lost and disoriented inside this wreck. Penetration is not advised. Cable leads off the wreck. The crane is about 100 feet east of the barge. Many fishermen frequent this area.

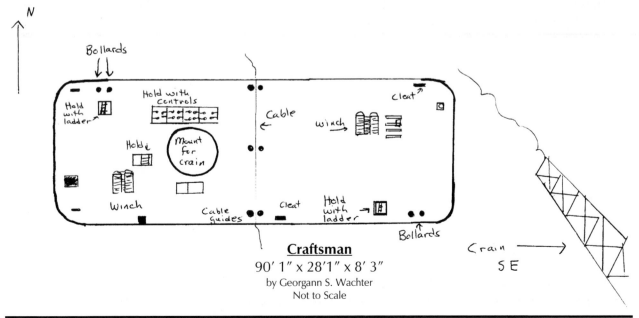

Craftsman
90' 1" x 28'1" x 8' 3"
by Georgann S. Wachter
Not to Scale

CHARLES H. DAVIS

Official #: 34107   **Site #:** 28

Location: 1 mile north of Cleveland Harbor

Coordinates: TD: 43778.6 57475.7   DGPS: 41 30.780   81 43.521

Lies: bow northeast   **Depth:** 40 feet

Type: propeller   **Cargo:** stone

Power: 165 hoursepower steeple compound engine

Owner(s) E.W. Haskins of Saginaw, Michigan

Built: 1881 at Saginaw, Michigan

Dimensions: 145′ x 31′ x 9′   **Tonnage:** 390 gross   333 net

Date of Loss: Saturday, June 13, 1903

Cause of Loss: foundered in storm

Charles H. Davis
Historical Collections of the Great Lakes

Story of the Loss:

The *Charles H. Davis* was bound for Cleveland with a load of stone from Kelleys Island. A northwest gale caused her destruction. However, the aging *Davis* had been built of pine and was not as sturdy as her oaken brethren. In addition she was overloaded with stone when she left the quarries at Kelleys Island. While this was in accordance with the practice of the day, the overburdened ship was in trouble from the start of her voyage. "Although in serious trouble the *Davis* made good weather until close to the breakwater. Here she encountered the backwash and the third large wave which boarded the boat caused the cargo to shift (Detroit Free Press, June 14, 1903)." By the time she was in sight of Cleveland, the *Davis* has shipped a great deal of water and was riding very low to the waterline. She blew signals of distress. Several tugs went to the rescue and were standing as wave after wave washed over the foundering ship. The final wave to come abroad overwhelmed the *Davis* and she sank, throwing her crew into the water. Six men and a woman were rescued by the tugs. However, in the confusion of the moment, no one checked to be sure everyone had been pulled from the water. On returning to shore, tugs *Frank W* and *William Kennedy* found that neither of them had saved Captain E.W. Haskins.

From the *Detroit Free Press*, June 14, 1903:

TO THE BOTTOM LIKE A STONE

STEAMER DAVIS SANK WITHIN SIGHT OF CLEVELAND HARBOR

CAPT. HASKINS LOST. SEVEN OF CREW WERE SAVED

While the little steamer Charles H. Davis, heavily laden with stone from Kelleys Island, was trying to make the opening of the breakwater this afternoon she was boarded by several heavy seas, became unmanageable and foundered, going to the bottom like a stone, and leaving the members of the crew clinging to bits of wreckage and the battered and swamped life boat.

This was the second small vessel to go down within sight of the breakwater within as many days. Capt. E. W. Haskins, who was also the owner, went down with it. The remaining members of the crew, six men and a woman, were rescued by tugs and the lifesaving crew.

Although in serious trouble, the Davis made good weather until close to the breakwater. Here she encountered the backwash and the third large wave which boarded the boat caused the cargo to shift. The next sea which went aboard was fatal and the craft went to the bottom. When she came within sight of the harbor signals of distress were blown and several tugs went to the rescue and were close at hand when the tug went down.

The Wreck Today:

This wreck sits very close to the main channel entering Cleveland Harbor. All that remains of the *Davis* is her boiler, a small pony boiler, and a broken up pile of boards. The bottom is heavily silted and the visibility is often poor.

CAUTION: Watch for heavy boat and freighter traffic!

Dominion

Official #:　　　　　　　　　　　　　　　　**Site #:**　60

Location:　5.3 miles south of Wheatley Harbor, Ontario

Coordinates:　LORAN: 43880.9　57218.2　　　DGPS: 41 59.750　82 26.738

Lies:　east/west　　　　　　　　　　　　　　**Depth:**　45 feet

Type:　dredge　　　　　　　　　　　　　　　**Cargo:**　steam dredge

Power:　towed

Owner(s)　Conlon Brothers, Thorold, Ontario

Built:

Dimensions:　approximately 75' x 25'　　　　**Tonnage:**

Date of Loss:　Friday, October 28, 1892

Cause of Loss:　capsized while under tow

Dominion

Barge similar to the Dominion
Great Lakes Historical Society

Story of the Loss:

The dredge barge *Dominion* and six scows were under tow by the tugs *Home Rule*, *Georgia*, and *C.J.G. Munroe* when the lake whipped into a frenzy. After leaving Port Colborne, the tow got in trouble off Port Burwell and the barges were lost. The following day the scows were recovered but bad wether continued to plague the convoy and they tried to seek shelter under Pelee Point. Once under the point, the wind shifted and, without shelter from the gale, the *Dominion* was lost.

The crew of the dredge was rescued, and the six scows also under tow by the tugs were cast adrift but recovered the following day.

It should be noted that, as is often the case, there is great confusion in contemporary newspaper accounts on the name of the dredge. It is variously called the *Niagara*, *Dominion*, and *Domain*. In addition to the *Dominion*, Conlon owned a schooner named *Niagara* and a lake barge named *Maggie*.

The Wreck Today:

The *Dominion* is located on a rock and sand bottom. Coal that fired her steam boiler lays scattered about. Near the boiler are china shards and on the starboard side are large "C" clamps. The stern is broken. Chain lays wrapped around the winch.

Large C-clamps adorn the murky waters.

Round Eyed Gobies abound at the site.

A pitcher and broken bottle are among the many artifacts.

Videocapture of the Dominion by Mike Wachter

GEORGE DUNBAR

Official #: 10890   **Site #:** 70

Location: 8 miles NE of Kelleys Island

Coordinates: LORAN: 43729.6 57076.4   DGPS: 41 40.631   82 33.893

Lies: bow southeast   **Depth:** 45 feet

Type: propeller   **Cargo:** Coal

Power: steam engine

Owner(s) Saginaw Bay Transportation Company

Built: 1867 in Allegan, Michigan by A. McMillan

Dimensions: 133.5' x 25.3' x 9.1'   **Tonnage:** 238 gross 190 net

Date of Loss: Sunday, June 29, 1902

Cause of Loss: sprung a leak in storm

Sidescan Image of the wreck of the George Dunbar
Aqua Vision Research

George Dunbar Name Board
Photo by Georgann Wachter

Story of the Loss:

The story of the loss of the *George Dunbar* is one of great tragedy and even greater heroism on Lake Erie. By the time of her loss she had been converted from a steam barge to a tow barge and then back to a steam barge. On her final voyage, she was traveling from Cleveland, Ohio to Alpena, Michigan with a cargo of coal. She began leaking after encountering a fierce storm. The water in her holds continued to rise as the crew worked valiantly to stem the tide. As the ship continued to take on water, Captain John Little gave the order to abandon ship. Five of his seven man crew refused to take to the lifeboat in the heavy seas. The captain, his wife, daughter, and the other two crewmen took the yawl boat. As the ship succumbed to the sea, the remaining five crewmen were forced to a life raft. Unfortunately, they could not stay afloat in the tormented sea, and all five drowned. Meanwhile, partway to shore, the yawl boat capsized. The two crewmen aboard were without lifejackets and they were never seen again. The captain and his family were left bobbing in their lifejackets. Fortunately, as they were carried by the waves, residents of Kelleys Island sighted them. Most of the observers believed there was no way to save the struggling family. However, the islanders helped launched a small, flat bottomed skiff and Fred Dishinger, his son Fred, Jr. and Mayor James Hamilton rowed to reach the struggling family. Only a fool or a hero would brave such waves in a flat bottomed skiff. The waves washed over their rowboat and required them to bail constantly or risk being capsized in the storm tossed waters. On reaching the family, they realized they could not bring them into the boat without overturning it. A line was secured to Captain Little and all three were towed to shore.

Fred Dishinger, Fred Dishinger, Jr. and Mayor James Hamilton received a U.S. Government medal for their heroism.

The Wreck Today:

The Dunbar lies in the mud at a depth of 45 feet. The most remarkable features of the wreck are her windlass and donkey boiler. Her stack lies approximately forty feet off her stern. The name board of the *Dunbar* washed up on Kelleys Island and is now on display at the Great Lakes Historical Society Museum, Vermilion, Ohio. The Historical Society also displays side scan images of this site in their Lake Erie Shipwreck Research Center.

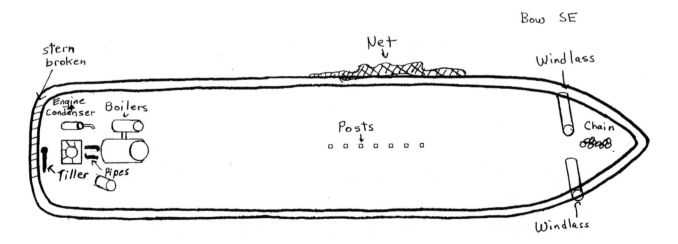

George Dunbar
133'5" x 25'3" x 9'1"
by Georgann S. Wachter
Not to Scale

DUNDEE

Official #:	157366	**Site #:**	25
Location:	14 miles north of Rocky River, Ohio		
Coordinates:	LORAN: 43841.0 57456.5	DGPS: 41 41.330 81 50.634	
Lies:	130° x 310° bow northwest	**Depth:**	75 feet
Type:	schooner – barge	**Cargo:**	iron ore
Power:	sail – towed		
Owner(s)	Nicholas Transit Company; Kinsman Transit Company		
Built:	1893 at West Bay City, Michigan by James Davidson Shipyard Hull #54		
Dimensions:	211' x 35' x 16'5"	**Tonnage:**	1043 gross 991 net
Date of Loss:	Tuesday, September 11, 1900		
Cause of Loss:	foundered in storm		

Dundee

Ralph Roberts' Collection

Story of the Loss:

The *Dundee* entered service in 1893, at the beginning of the Great Depression and was lost in 1900, the year the Great Depression ended. She carried bulk cargo to many ports on the Great Lakes providing raw materials for commerce in the very worst of economic times. She had a capacity for 375,000 board feet of lumber.

Downbound in the tow of the steamer *John N. Glidden*, the Dundee carried iron ore for Ashtabula, Ohio. Shortly before midnight on September 11th a strong gale came cross the lake and, as was the custom at the time, the *Glidden* set the *Dundee* free to fend for herself. Struggling to keep his ship on course, Captain Martin Elnen believed the ship would make it. However, all hope was lost when a deafening torrent of water all but buried the schooner. After this wash of sea, the mate ran to the captain to advise him the ship had lost her rudder and two feet of water were in the hold. As the storm swept the female cook to sea, Captain Elnen and five crewmen climbed the rigging of the wildly tossing boat. Hours later, the steamer *Tower* found the six survivors lashed to the top masts and took them to safety.

The *John B. Lyons* sank off Conneaut, Ohio, the same day.

The Wreck Today:

Upright in 75 feet of water, the *Dundee* is an awesome sight. Her stern is broken off and six large cargo hatches make penetration of the wreck easy and relatively safe. However, several feet of silt in the holds are easily stirred up, dramatically reducing visibility. Also, the bow has begun to collapse and deck machinery has fallen into the hold in recent years. Care must be taken on this aging wreck! You'll find the windlass, some anchor chain, a donkey boiler, and turnbuckles that held the rigging.

One of the *Dundee's* anchors is in the parking lot outside the Cargo Warehouse in Vermilion, Ohio.

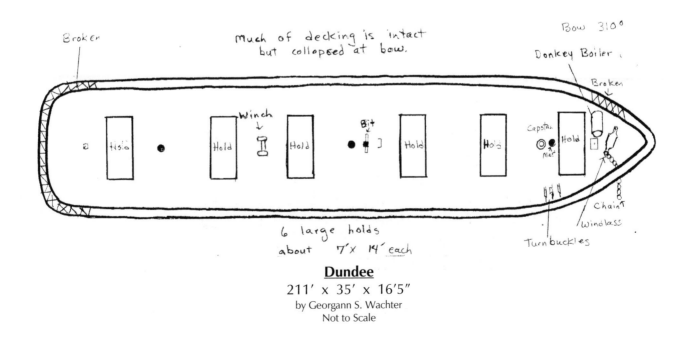

Dundee
211' x 35' x 16'5"
by Georgann S. Wachter
Not to Scale

ERIEAU QUARRY STONE

Official #:   **Site #:**   15

Location: just east of the Rondeau Bay breakwall

Coordinates: LORAN: 44072.6   57559.3   DGPS: 42 15.412   81 54.341

Lies: east - west   **Depth:**   16 feet

Type: wood barge   **Cargo:**   quarry stone

Power:

Owner(s)

Built:

Dimensions: **Tonnage:**

Date of Loss:

Cause of Loss:

Story of the Loss:

Unknown.   This site is locally known as **"Brian's Wreck"**.

The Wreck Today:

Silting, heavy boat traffic, and nearby pilings make this a tricky dive. Large cut quarry blocks, probably destined for the breakwall, lie on the silty bottom.

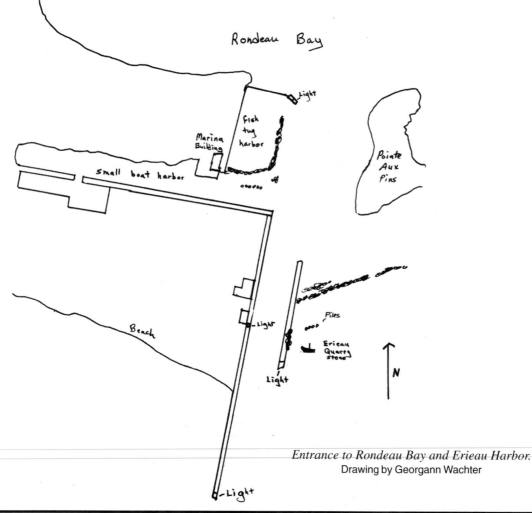

Entrance to Rondeau Bay and Erieau Harbor.
Drawing by Georgann Wachter

EXCHANGE

Official #:	7315	**Site #:**	89
Location:	200 feet south of Kelleys Island		
Coordinates:	LORAN: 43672.2 56974.0	DGPS: 41 35.643 82 43.231	
Lies:	scattered	**Depth:**	15 feet
Type:	schooner	**Cargo:**	stone
Power:	sail		
Owner(s)	James Lawler of Sandusky		
Built:	1857 at Vermilion, Ohio by I. W. Nicholas		
Dimensions:	138' x 26' x 11'8"	**Tonnage:**	292.04
Date of Loss:	Saturday, November 21, 1874		
Cause of Loss:	grounded		

Story of the Loss:

The winds of November are notorious on the Great Lakes. The howling winds and raging seas of a November storm have caused the loss of a great many vessels on our inland seas. While, the winds were strong and good for sailing, there was no storm to cause the loss of the sailing vessel *Exchange*. On Friday, November 20, 1874, there was a moderate wind and no storm. And, even in their silence, the winds of November managed to bring and end to the *Exchange*!

She had taken on a load of stone at Kelleys Island Middle Dock. Thinking they were fortunate to be making a late season run in mild weather, Captain Lawler and crew set sail to make way into a strong wind from the southwest. They were bound for Cleveland with approximately one hundred cords of stone. As they rounded the corner of Kelleys Island, the main halyards gave way, leaving the crew with no control of the sails. As the crew worked to regain control of the sails and their ship, the *Exchange* was pushed before the wind. Before they could make way, the vessel literally drifted into shoal water off the old railroad dock. She struck hard and settled immediately to the bottom.

Unable to free their ship, Captain Lawler and crew took refuge in the home of Mr. George Bristol, superintendent of the Kelley Quarries. With Mr. Bristol's assistance the cabin furnishings and the Captains personal belongings were removed from the wreck. A few days later, she was abandoned. The following spring, the tug *Winslow* took six steam pumps to the island and tried to raise her. Much of the stone weighing the vessel down was removed from her holds and the pumps lowered the water level considerably. However, further inspection revealed the damage was too severe to warrant raising the vessel.

Once the ice and storms attacked her she became a hazard. In May of 1884 the steam barge *Thrio*, the yacht *Olive*, an unnamed scow and barge all became victims of the now submerged *Exchange*. As a result, a plea was issued for the removal of much of the vessel.

The Wreck Today:

Located on a weed covered rock bottom, there is not much left at this shallow water site other than the anchor chain and some timbers. This wreck is occasionally done as a shore dive. However, the properties adjacent to the wreck site are privately owned and permission is needed to cross the property and enter the water.

Watch for heavy boat traffic, including the ferryboat dock to the west.

D. L. FILER

Official #: 35311   **Site #:** 101

Location: 3 1/2 miles east of Bar Point Light

Coordinates:

Lies: **Depth:** 18 feet

Type: wood barge   **Cargo:** coal

Power: towed

Owner(s) Hamilton Transportation Company, Chicago, Illinois

Built: 1871 at Manistee, Michigan by P. Barlow

Dimensions: 156'6" x 30' x 10'   **Tonnage:** 357 gross 339 net

Date of Loss: Friday, October 20, 1916

Cause of Loss: foundered

D. L. Filer
Author's Collection

Story of the Loss:

With the sound of a band in the background and flags waving in the breeze, the *D. L. Filer* was launched on a nippy May day in 1871. Roughly 400 people gathered on her decks for the uncomfortable bumpy ride as the *Caroline Williams* towed her into Lake Michigan. The *Filer* was named for Delos L. Filer, a lumberman, local doctor, and government official.

In what was, perhaps, a portent of things to come, the barge sank in Lake Michigan in October 1898. After hanging in the rigging for twenty four hours, her crew was rescued by the Racine, Wisconsin lifesavers. She was raised to sail for 18 more years before meeting her end in the "Black Friday" storm of October 1916. This famous storm took a severe toll on Lake Erie. Four ships were lost. One entire crew went to their deaths while on two other vessels only the captain survived.

The steam barge *Tempest* had departed Buffalo, New York with the barges *D.L. Filer* and *Interlaken* as consorts. Caught in the raging storm and agonizingly close to the safety of the Detroit River, the *Filer* and *Interlaken* were cast off. The aged *Filer* anchored in an attempt to ride out the storm. However, she began to leak. As she filled with water, six men clambered up the forward mast while Captain John Mattison took to the stern mast alone. Under the weight of the crew, the foremast fell, plunging the six sailors into the frigid water. Only Oscar Johanson was able to make it to the aft mast to join the captain. Through the long, dark, stormy night, the two clung to the mast. At least one vessel, unaware of their plight, passed them by.

In the early hours of Saturday morning the lookout on the downbound steamer *Western States* spotted the men perched above the waves. Captain Robinson brought his ship as close as possible to the two men hanging in the rigging. However, as a boat was lowered, the numbing cold overcame Johanson and he slipped into the sea. Captain John Mattison was rescued and taken to Amhursburg, Ontario. There, he carried out the sad duty of daily searching for his lost crew.

The Wreck Today:

The *D. L. Filer's* remains have not been found. Records indicate that she may have been removed as a hazard to navigation.

FLEETWOOD (BRICK WRECK)

Official #: 81145   **Site #:** 18

Location: 20 miles southwest of Erieau, Ontario

Coordinates: LORAN: 43942.0 57414.4   DGPS: 42 00.183 82 04.216

Lies: bow north   **Depth:** 77 feet

Type: propeller   **Cargo:** light

Power: triple expansion steam engine with two scotch boilers

Owner(s) Nicholson Transit Company

Built: 1887 at West Bay City, Michigan by F.W. Wheeler & Company

Dimensions: 265'5" x 40'6" x 19'4"   **Tonnage:** 1687 gross 1175 net

Date of Loss: 1931?

Cause of Loss: scuttled

Fleetwood

Great Lakes Historical Society

Story of the Loss:

Originally christened as the bulk freighter *William H. Gratwick*, in 1918 she was converted to an automobile carrier and renamed *Fleetwood*. After this rebuild, she transported new cars from Detroit, Michigan to ports throughout the Great Lakes. Regrettably, the depression years proved to be too much for this ageing vessel. She was abandoned in 1926 and stripped of her machinery at Ecorse, Michigan. The *Roumania*, which had been built the same year as the *Fleetwood*, was abandoned and stripped at the same time. In fact, the *Fleetwood* and *Roumania* had two of the first three triple expansion engines on the Great Lakes. After the *Fleetwood* and *Roumania* were stripped they were sold for building docks. The *Fleetwood* was to go to Buffalo, New York and the *Roumania* was bound for Cleveland, Ohio.

Both vessels left Ecorse in tow of the aging steamer *Fellowcraft*. Somehow, while traversing a calm lake, the *Fellowcraft* reported losing both her tows when the hulls mysteriously foundered. The foundering came suddenly and without warning somewhere in the vicinity of Southeast Shoal. Captain Bert Bourassa, in command of the *Fellowcraft*, reportedly "forgot" to log the time when the small convoy passed Southeast Shoal Light. As a result, they were never found. Suspicion at the time was the captain had intentionally scuttled the two hulls rather than incur the expense of towing them to Cleveland and Buffalo.

The Wreck Today:

The site is commonly known in Canada as the "Light Wreck" because the divers who found her lost their dive lights while diving the wreck. The area where her firebox would have been is still paved with bricks. This particular feature leads to the US divers calling her the "Brick Wreck" and, these bricks gave the first clue to identifying the wreck. The bricks are inscribed "Hallwood Block, PAT. , A.P. Green F.B.C. (fire brick company), Crown D.P. (dry press)" A.P. Green began business in 1910. The bricks were probably installed in 1918 when the *Fleetwood* was converted to an auto carrier.

There are two rows of ships knees along the wrecks fallen sides, indicating that this ship was a two deck propeller. Part of the starboard bow is broken. She has a curved stern and huge rudder. The vessel appears to have been filled with river stone and scuttled. All of her machinery has been removed.

S. F. GALE

Official #:	22343	**Site #:**	23
Location:	18 miles northwest of Cleveland, Ohio		
Coordinates:	LORAN: 43858.6 57449.4	DGPS: 41 44.455 81 52.922	
Lies:	bow southwest	**Depth:**	78 feet
Type:	schooner - 2 masts	**Cargo:**	stone
Power:	sail		
Owner(s)	Captain Billson		
Built:	1847 at Chicago, Illinois by James Averill		
Dimensions:	122' 6" x 24' x 9'9"	**Tonnage:**	225.34 gross
Date of Loss:	Tuesday, November 28, 1876		
Cause of Loss:	foundered		

Story of the Loss:

Originally built as a brig, the *Gale* was changed to schooner in 1870. She served in the grain trade for many years.

The *Gale* was bound from Kelleys Island to Erie, Pennsylvania with a load of stone when she foundered in a storm with all hands. Her cabin, trunks with ladies clothing and her books washed ashore near Fairport. She was first reported sunk by Captain Averill of the scow-schooner *Charles Crawford*, who came upon the spars of the sunken vessel.

From the *Cleveland Herald*, December 5, 1876:

THE LOST SCHOONER

The Vessel Sunk off this Port is the Schooner S. F. Gale.

Since last Thursday rumors have been in circulation along the docks that a vessel was sunk about sixteen miles off this port in a northerly direction. It was first reported by the scow-schooner *Charles Crawford,* which arrived here on that day from Sand Beach, on Lake Huron. The captain stated that about eight o'clock that morning he passed the spars of a sunken vessel, giving the distance away as above stated. Since then various rumors have been afloat regarding the craft, what one it was, where she was bound, etc. As several Cleveland vessels, and among them the S. F. *Gale,* were over due at this and other ports on Lake Erie, they were connected with the lost craft, and, in turn, each was re-ported as being the unfortunate one. Within the past *few* days, however it has been definitely settled in the minds of many that the *Gale* was the doomed one. Yesterday a dispatched was received at this office, from Fairport, which states that: "The books of the S. F. *Gale* came ashore last Thursday night at the headlands west of Fairport, at the same point where other parts of a wreck were washed ashore the day previous." There can be no doubt but every person on the vessel was lost. The *Gale* cleared from this port November 13th for Port Stanley, with a load of coal. From there she went to Kelley Island and took on board a load of lime and stone for Erie. She was rated as a fair vessel, and Captain Billson, her commander and owner, was a man respected by all who knew him.

On Sunday there was a report that a vessel was sunk off Fairport. But it was probably occasioned by the fact that a portion of the wreck of the *Gale* washed ashore there, and as no name was attached by which the identity could be made known, it was supposed to be some other craft.

The Wreck Today:

The *Gale* is sunk in the mud with her stern partially collapsed. Starting at the bow, the diver will come across the windlass, anchor chain, small hatch with ladder, small machinery, pump, and the rudder. Deadeyes are still in place along her sides. There is a stove on the port side stern in the cabin area.

Early divers on this wreck tell tales of finding human remains wearing a large pea coat tangled in the rigging and clutching the bones of a cat. Based on the size of the buckled shoes they found, he was a very large man. In the pea coat pockets were both live and spent gun shells. This finding had the divers imagining the skipper forcing the crew to man the pumps at gunpoint while attempting to save his cat. Who knows, maybe it is true.

S. F. Gale
122' 6" x 24' x 9'9"
by Georgann S. Wachter
Not to Scale

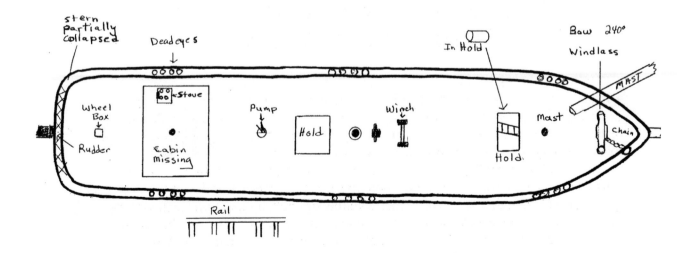

E.K. Gilbert (Bow Cabin)

Official #: 7238   **Site #:** 56

Location: 13 miles northeast of Pelee Point

Coordinates: LORAN: 43892.6 57315.0   DGPS: 41 56.811   82 14.107

Lies: bow west   **Depth:** 70 feet

Type: schooner   **Cargo:** coal

Power: 2 masted sail

Owner(s) Stevenson of Detroit

Built: 1855 at Saint Clair, Michigan by William S. Redfield

Dimensions: 92'6" x 23'6" x 8'4"   **Tonnage:** 162

Date of Loss: November 11, 1868

Cause of Loss: leaked

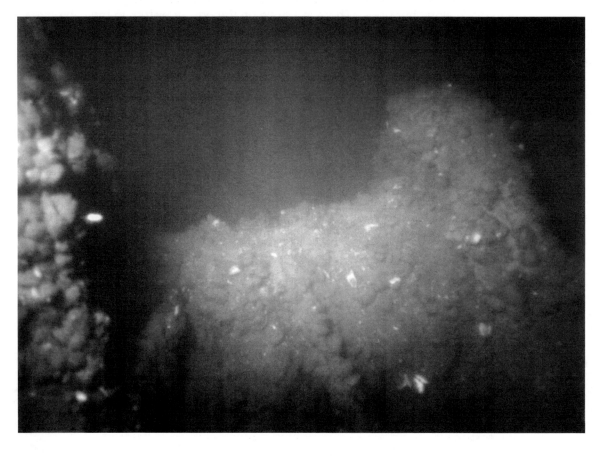

Windlass on the E.K. Gilbert
Georgann Wachter

Story of the Loss:

This site is commonly known as the "Bow Cabin Wreck". Although the identity of the wreck has not been confirmed, we believe this shipwreck to be the *E.K. Gilbert*.

The *Gilbert* was bound from Cleveland, Ohio to Detroit, Michigan. She was loaded with coal at the time of her loss. On November 11, 1868 she sprung a leak that overwhelmed the crew's ability to pump the water out faster than water was entering the vessel. She became a total loss.

Our tentative identification of this site as the *E.K. Gilbert* is based on the ships dimensions, cargo, and construction; as well as dating of a jug recovered from the wreck site by divers from Save Ontario Shipwrecks. With her stern missing, on site measurements show the vessel to be approximately 91' x 23'. This is an excellent fit to the Gilbert's measurement of 92'6" x 23'6". Other characteristics of the wreck match the design of the *E. K. Gilbert*. We traced a jug recovered from the site to a wholesale liquor dealer, Sylvester F. Eagan of Buffalo, New York. Eagan began his business in 1867.

The Wreck Today:

Sitting upright in the mud with her bow pointed westward, this vessel had two masts. The rails of the wreck disappear into the bottom silt, as the stern is either missing or buried in the silt. She rises only 4 feet above the silt line.

Artifacts on the wreck include a winch, capstan, bilge pump, windlass, chain, stove, storm anchor, wood blocks, and dead eyes. The wreck has some fish net on it, so exercise caution.

E.K. Gilbert (Bow Cabin)
92'6" x 23'6" x 8'4"
by Georgann S. Wachter
Not to Scale

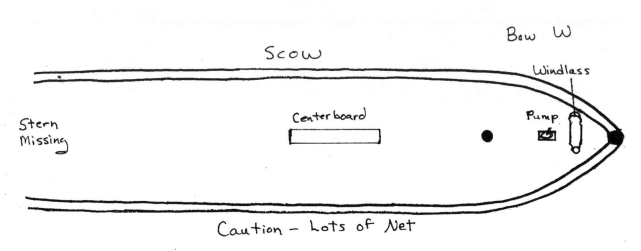

JAY GOULD

Official #: 75117   **Site #:** 65

Location: 5 miles SE of Point Pelee

Coordinates: LORAN: 43829.2 57202.6   DGPS: 41 51.531 82 24.596

Lies: bow east   **Depth:** 45 feet

Type: propeller bulk freighter   **Cargo:** coal

Power: steeple compound steam engine

Owner(s) Rochester Transit Company

Built: 1869 at Buffalo, New York by Mason & Bidwell

Dimensions: 213'8" x 33'9" x 11'5"   **Tonnage:** 840 gross 523 net

Date of Loss: Monday, June 17, 1918

Cause of Loss: sprung a leak & foundered

Jay Gould
Great Lakes Historical Society

Story of the Loss:

Bound from Cleveland, Ohio for Sandwich, Ontario, the *Jay Gould* towed the barge *Commodore* through a bruising Lake Erie storm. Losing the battle with the storm, the *Gould* took on water and foundered southeast of Pelee Point. The passing steamer *Midvale* rescued the crew and transported them to Ashtabula, Ohio.

Set free to fend for itself, the barge *Commadore* also foundered. Her seven crew members were rescued by the steamer *Mataafa*.

The Wreck Today:

Located on hard pack bottom in chilly water. There are two capstans, propeller, engine, boiler, chain, and lots of wood. There is net off the port side and occasional current. An excellent survey of this site was developed by Save Ontario Shipwrecks, Windsor.

Sidescan image of the wreck of the Jay Gould. Image by Aqua Vision Research

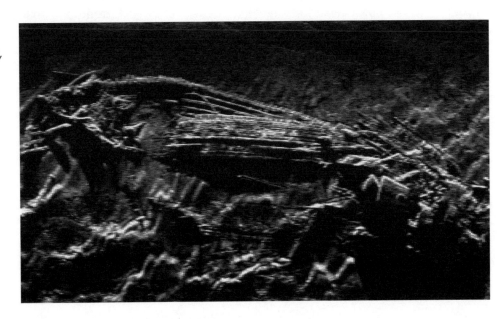

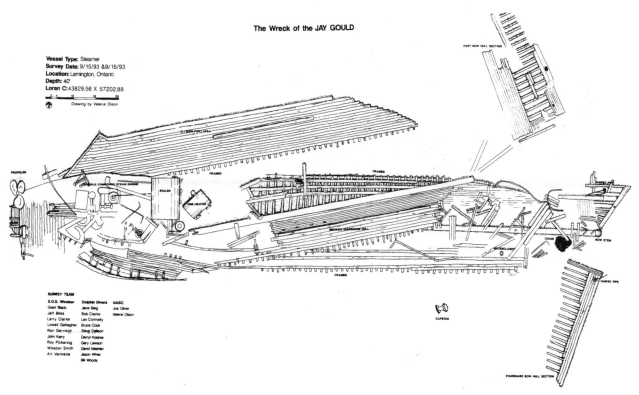

Save Ontario Shipwrecks site survey of the Jay Gould conducted September 15 & 16, 1993

GRAND TRAVERSE

Official #: 91129   **Site #:** 97

Location: 3 miles southeast of Colchester, Ontario

Coordinates: LORAN: 43795.9   56975.1   DGPS: 41 56.903   82 53.678

Lies: **Depth:** 40 feet

Type: propeller   **Cargo:** coal, barrels of apples, fish,

Power: steam   and cider

Owner(s) M.M. Drake, Buffalo, New York

Built: 1879 at Marine City, Michigan by Morley and Hill

Dimensions: 181'2" x 33' x 14'1"   **Tonnage:** 869.68 gross 749.18 net

Date of Loss: Monday, October 19, 1896

Cause of Loss: collision

Grand Traverse
Historical Collections of the Great Lakes

Story of the Loss:

Originally named *Morley*, the name was changed to *Grand Traverse* in 1886 when she was rebuilt. The *Morley* was almost lost at Grand Marais, Lake Superior when she spent the winter locked in ice. Once released from the ice she was rebuilt and renamed.

At 5:00 a.m. the *Grand Traverse* and the composite steamer *Livingston* collided. The *Grand Traverse* was bound from Buffalo, New York to Green Bay, Wisconsin and the *Livingston* carried corn from Chicago, Illinois to Buffalo. Following the collision, the crewmembers of both boats refused to tell the story of the collision. It seems they had been ordered by their owners and agents to keep quiet until the incident came to trial or was settled for damages. The October 29, 1896 *Detroit Free Press* reported: "It is impossible to ascertain the details of the steering and the exchange of signals, as this is the important point that gives a line to the conduct of the men on watch, determining largely which was to blame." Both first mates were in command at the time of the collision and, as might be expected, blamed each other.

The *Livingston* hit the *Grand Traverse* with such force that her bow was buried three fourths of the way into the keel of the *Grand Traverse*. Most of the crew of the *Grand Traverse* were in their bunks below decks at the time of the collision. Donning minimal clothing in great haste, they scrambled from their beds as the *Livingston* kept her nose buried in the small steamer. Most were able to climb ladders to the *Livingston*. Others scrambled to the texas deck in hopes it would still be above water after the steamer settled to the bottom of the lake. To their good fortune, the texas remained above water and all were rescued after the little steamer sank. The *Livingston* took Captain Kelly and his crew to Detroit.

The sailors on the *Grand Traverse* lost everything on the boat and were given transportation back to Buffalo.

The Wreck Today:

The wreck is badly broken up on a silty bottom. Her engine and much of her machinery were salvaged. Good visibility on this wreck is very unusual. However, rumor has it that the barrels of apples are still aboard her!

John B. Griffin

Official #: 75635   **Site #:** 33

Location: 2 miles off Lakewood, Ohio

Coordinates: LORAN: 43767.1   57427.4   DGPS: 41 31.093   81 49.176

Lies: bow east   **Depth:** 50 feet

Type: tug   **Cargo:** light

Power: steam engine

Owner(s) W. A. Creech, Manager, Independent Tug Line

Built: 1874 at Buffalo, New York by Carroll

Dimensions: 57'4" x 14'6" x 6'8"   **Tonnage:** 28.21 gross   14.11 net

Date of Loss: Tuesday, July 12, 1892

Cause of Loss: fire

John B. Griffin
C. Patrick Labadie Collection

Story of the Loss:

Traveling in the dead of night, the *John B. Griffin* was two miles off of Rocky River, Ohio when, at 1:00 in the morning, she caught fire. Her crew of three, Captain Charles Donahue, engineer John Abbott, and fireman William Reed, narrowly escaped with their lives. As soon as the flames were discovered, Captain Donahue headed the boat for shore. However, the flames spread so rapidly that the crew was forced to abandon ship before reaching the safety of shallow water. As the flames engulfed them, the men threw the life raft overboard and jumped in after it. As they swam about one mile to shore, the tug burned to the waterline and sank.

Although the crew escaped with their lives, nothing else was saved from the tug.

The Wreck Today:

This wreck lists to starboard on a mud bottom. The most notable features of the wreck are her boiler, pony boiler, rudder, and stack.

G. P. GRIFFITH

Official #:   **Site #:**   9

Location: 3 miles west of the Chagrin River, Willowick, Ohio

Coordinates: LORAN: GPS: bell recovered at: 41 38.945   81 28.672

                                          PA: of charred remains: 41 41.233   81 26.194

Lies: scattered   **Depth:**   20-30 feet

Type: paddle wheel steamer   **Cargo:**   passengers; English, German,

Power: cross head engine with 31' diameter paddle wheels   and Irish immigrants

Owner(s)   Richard Sears & others

Built: 1847 at Maumee City, Ohio by David R. Stebbins

Dimensions: 193'3" x 28'1" x 11'3"   **Tonnage:**   587

Date of Loss: Monday, June 17, 1850

Cause of Loss: fire

G. P. Griffith
Great Lakes Historical Society

Story of the Loss:

The burning of the *G.P. Griffith* ranks as the third worst loss of life disaster on the Great Lakes. Only one child and one woman survived the disaster that claimed 230 to 290 lives. Many of the immigrant women aboard were burdened with heavy garments, which often concealed gold to start lives in the new world.

In his notebook dated 1840-1850, Jonathan Coolidge, Lake County Commissioner of Wrecks, lists hundreds of items recovered from the *Griffith* and stored in Buchard's barn. Some items listed were: 1 old blue frock coat, 2 pair woolen pants, 1 coarse linen shirt marked S.B., 1 large German chest - damaged, 20 silk handkerchiefs of various kinds, 1 piece of military horse equipage, 13 pocket knives, 1 pocket flask, 10 bonnets - all worthless, 2 miniature portraits, 2 catholic prayer books, 1 fiddle bow.

A letter from the Lake County Historical Society fixes blame on Captain Roby of the *Griffith*: *"My stepfather was the Lake County Coroner when the Griffith burned. He told me that he did not arrive on the scene until the middle of the afternoon, and all the rescued bodies had been carried up the bank and laid in rows. He said decomposition had already begun and the stench made a hasty burial imperative. ... He said the boat was on fire after leaving Fairport. The captain was drunk and determined to run it to Cleveland. The fire developed so rapidly that the steamer was steered ashore at Willoughby, with the result that is history."* The letter is signed, Arthur D. Coe, Euclid, Ohio, August 11, 1921.

At 3:00 a.m. an alarm was given that fire had broken out between the stacks. The cause is believed to be a new, highly flammable, engine oil. The result was disastrous.

Captain C.C. Roby immediately steered the vessel toward shore. She grounded one half mile out on a sand bar. As the flames enveloped the vessel, all on board were exhorted to save themselves. In the ensuing panic, families flung themselves in the lake. Women, in their heavy garments, which often concealed gold for the new world, faired the worst. In fact, the only woman to survive was the barber's wife! The captain, who was on his first trip, was lost with his wife and child. Many struggled, grasping at each other. About 40 of the 300 passengers and 30 crew made it safely to the beach. Many of the bodies were buried in trenches on the beach.

The Wreck Today:

Divers have visited the rock strewn sandy resting place of the *Griffith* for years. The debris is widely scattered and the 300 pound bell was recovered in 30 feet of water. The GPS location given is the site where the bell was recovered. The propeller *Delaware* dragged the boat into 10 feet of water where remains of the unburned hull, some machinery, outside planks, timbers, and portions of the wheel may be found. Two years later some of her engine parts were salvaged.

Brass spikes from her hull are on display at the Lake County Historical Society. In June 2000 a marker memorializing those lost in the disaster was unveiled in Willowick Lakefront Lodge Park.

Caution: heavy boat traffic.

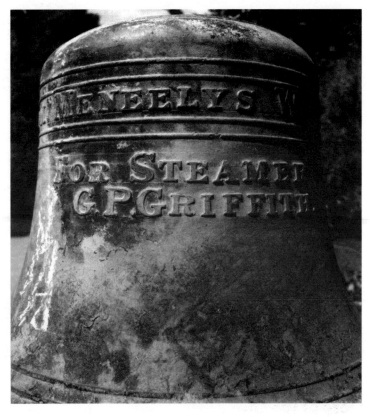

Bell of the G. P. Griffith was recoved by divers in 1974. Authors' Collection

W.R. Hanna

Official #: 26669   **Site #:** 87

Location: Kelleys Island North Bay

Coordinates: LORAN: 43688.2 57000.9   DGPS: 41 37.091 82 40.849

Lies: bow southwest   **Depth:** 8 feet

Type: scow   **Cargo:** stone

Power: sail

Owner(s) L.J. Seek of Toledo, Ohio

Built: 1857 at Sandusky, Ohio by William R. Hanna

Dimensions: 84.7' x 21.6' x 5.0'   **Tonnage:** 86.16 gross 81.86 net

Date of Loss: Thursday, October 14, 1886

Cause of Loss: storm

Kelleys Island Quarries Circa 1886
Remick Collection

Story of the Loss:

The *W.R. Hanna* was a square sterned scow. This small workhorse changed owners often in her short life and was wrecked in 1880 at South Beach, Michigan.

On October 14, 1886, the *W.R. Hanna* was loading stone at Kelleys Island Quarries. However, this Detroit bound cargo would never leave the waters of North Bay. Storm force winds swept the length and breadth of Lake Erie that day. They started blowing from the south at 30 to 40 miles per hour. As the day progressed the winds shifted southwest and built to 63 miles per hour. With winds averaging 55 miles per hour, the storm continued to rage through the night. In the midst of this blow sat the *Hanna*. She was partially loaded and being battered by the unrelenting wind and waves. Finally succumbing, she went ashore and was battered to pieces.

The *Hanna* was not the only vessel to fall victim to this devastating blow. The *Nevada* went aground at Ashtabula, Ohio. The *Belle Mitchell* and *George Case* were lost at Long Point. The *Saint Joseph* and *Sea Lark* were both stranded on Pelee Island. The *Star of Hope* was lost off Kelleys Island. And, the *O.M. Bond* was stranded below Rondeau Bay. All in all, it was not a good day to be on the lake.

The Wreck Today

The *W.R. Hanna* is located on a sand and rock bottom only a few yards from the wreck of the steamer *Adventure*. She lays parallel to shore with only 3-5 feet of clearance over her stone cargo.

There are stove parts to the west of her sternpost at the stern. Many artifacts have been removed from the wreck. These include jugs, tools, iron grindstones, and shoes.

CAUTION: This location has heavy boat traffic. The wreck lies very close to shore and the rocks in the area come very close to the surface.

Artifacts recovered from the W.R. Hanna were displayed at a recent archiology workshop. Georgann Wachter

HICKORY STICK

Official #:   267265   **Site #:**   46

Location: 3 miles north of Sheffield Lake, Ohio

Coordinates: LORAN: 43733.9 57282.9   DGPS: 41 32.301   82 06.236

Lies: northwest-southeast; crane is west of barge **Depth:**   55 feet

Type: dredge barge   **Cargo:**   crane

Power: towed

Owner(s)   Dyche Salvage Company, Lakewood, Ohio

Built: 1944 at New Rochelle, New York

Dimensions: 110' x 30' x 8'   **Tonnage:**   260

Date of Loss: Saturday, November 29, 1958

Cause of Loss: foundered

Hickory Stick
Fred Bultman

Story of the Loss:

Captain Dyche was a W.W.II Navy diver.

While being towed from Sandusky to Rocky River, Ohio by the tug *Black Marlin*, a storm with 75 mph winds caused the *Hickory Stick* to break free. According to Captain David A. Dyche, the six inch rope hawser between the tug and barge parted about 11:00 p.m. Friday. Recognizing the futility of saving his tow, Captain Dyche turned toward the safety of Lorain Harbor. Minutes later the *Black Marlin's* engines stopped. Coastguardsmen from Lorain station rescued the captain and frst mate Joseph Amberick, leaving the tug at anchor 4 miles northeast of Lorain. The tug later sank and has never been found.

At 3:00 a.m. Saturday, the cutter *Kaw* was dispatched from Coast Guard Station Cleveland to search for the barge. She was forced to return to harbor when icing knocked out her radar and threatened to make the vessel top heavy. Navy search planes from Gross Isle Navel station were also dispatched, but turned back due to unfavorable flying weather. Lorain Coast Guard found parts of the barge scattered for one to two miles along Avon Point.

The Wreck Today:

The wood and steal girders of the barge rise from a hard pack mud bottom. Tools, cooking implements, and other zebra mussel covered debris are scattered around the site. There is usually a line stretching west toward the boiler of the crane. Between the barge and crane are other metal wreck parts and an old hard hat compressor. Further west of the crane is the clam shell.

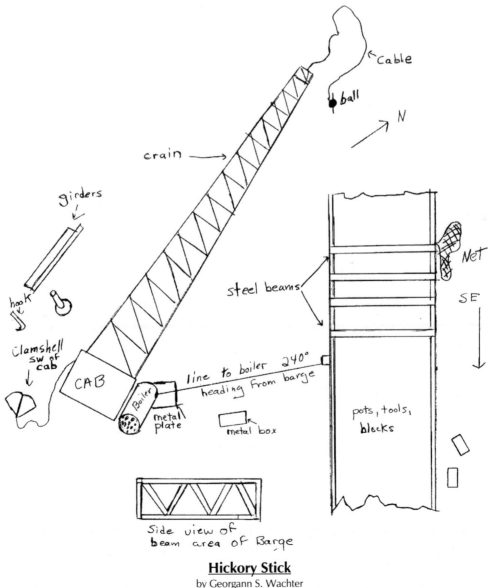

Hickory Stick
by Georgann S. Wachter
Not to Scale

IVANHOE

Official #:   **Site #:**   41

Location: 3 miles off Avon Lake, Ohio
Coordinates: LORAN: 43750.1   57316.9   DGPS: 41 33.310   82 02.826
Lies: bow southwest   **Depth:**   57 feet
Type: schooner   **Cargo:**   coal
Power: sail
Owner(s)
Built: 1848
Dimensions: 110' x 25'9" x 9'3"   **Tonnage:**   237
Date of Loss: Thursday, October 4, 1855
Cause of Loss: collision

Story of the Loss:

Known to local divers as the "Jug Wreck", this site is most likely the schooner *Ivanhoe*, of Buffalo, which was going from Cleveland to Mackinac, Michigan when she collided with the schooner *Arab*. The *Ivanhoe* sank while the *Arab* was only slightly damaged. The crew was rescued by the *Ohio*.

The Wreck Today:

The wreck sits on a mud bottom with her bow split and a slight list to port. The windlass is aboard her and the stern, with its rudder standing, seems almost separated from the wreck. Some decking remains near the centerboard on the port side, while the starboard rail is more intact.

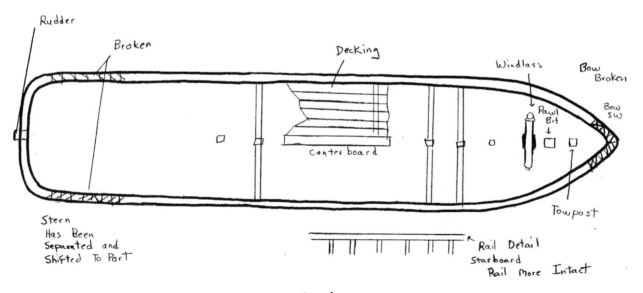

Ivanhoe
110' x 25'9" x 9'3"
by Georgann S. Wachter
Not to Scale

JACKIE'S WRECK

Official #:   **Site #:**   66

Location: 8 miles SE of Pelee Point

Coordinates: LORAN: 43839.4   57233.7   DGPS: 41 51.707   82 21.084

Lies: Bow northwest 330°   **Depth:**   50 feet

Type: Schooner two mast   **Cargo:**

Power: Sail

Owner(s)

Built:

Dimensions: Approximately 120'   **Tonnage:**

Date of Loss:

Cause of Loss:

Story of the Loss:

unknown

The Wreck Today:

Located on a mud bottom, *Jackie's Wreck* is flattened and her decking is gone as if she was salvaged. There are deadeyes and belaying pins. The centerboard is off the wreck.

Deadeye and strap recovered from the wreck of the Ivanhoe and displayed by Erie Diver's Museum.
Photo by Mike Wachter

FANNIE L. JONES

Official #: 37093   **Site #:** 29

Location: ¾ mile northwest of Cleveland Harbor

Coordinates: LORAN: 43777.0 57473.1   DGPS: 41 30.640 81 43.751

Lies: scattered   **Depth:** 36 feet

Type: scow/schooner   **Cargo:** limestone

Power: sail

Owner(s) John E. Wing of Kelleys Island Line Company and Captain E. C. Cummings of Milan, Ohio

Built: 1867 on the Black River at Lorain, Ohio by Root

Dimensions: 92'8" x 22'6" x 7'4"   **Tonnage:** 112.85 gross 107.23 net

Date of Loss: Sunday, August 10, 1890

Cause of Loss: foundered in storm

Story of the Loss:

The *Fannie L. Jones* set off from Kelleys Island "loaded down to the decks with stone." As she traveled to Ashtabula, Ohio to deliver stone for the new breakwall, a gale was blowing and the waves washed over the decks repeatedly. Captain Cummings decided to take shelter in Cleveland and ordered the crew to throw off part of the deck load and show a light for a tug. Very shortly after, with the vessel only a half mile from safety and the danger nearly behind them, the boat lurched. Crewmen Thomas Rafferty, William Smith, and Dan Thomas had no time to launch their boat and they took to the rigging. The captain sprang from the wheelhouse but was pulled down by the sinking ship. He was believed to have become tangled in the mainsail rigging and was unable to free himself.

At daybreak, the lifesaving lookout noticed masts sticking out of the water and alerted the rescue crew. Because of the storm, it took the lifesavers over an hour to reach the vessel. According to the Lifesaving Service Annual Report, "When they got there the main boom and gaff, with the sail attached were thrashing so violently through the action of the waves that it became necessary to approach very cautiously to avoid staving the boat." Interviews with the survivors indicated the loss was due to hatches being carelessly secured. The trip had begun in fair weather and the crew saw no reason to believe this would not continue. As the foul weather mounted, the poorly secured hatches permitted water in the holds. As the water rose, reducing the vessels buoyancy, her fate was soon sealed.

The crew of the *Fannie L. Jones* was rescued and provided dry clothing by the Women's National Relief Association.

The same storm that took the *Fannie Jones* also sank the schooner *Two Fannies* off of Bay Village, Ohio.

The Wreck Today:

The *Jones* lays scattered on a hard pack bottom. The sides are flattened and the bow is somewhat more intact. Boat traffic in this area is very heavy. Jugs recovered from the *Jones* are displayed at the Great Lakes Historical Society Inland Seas Museum in Vermilion, Ohio.

From the Chicago Inter Ocean, August 12, 1890:

MARINE INTELLIGENCE

Two Schooners Founder in Lake Erie off Cleveland Harbor.

Schooner Fannie L. Jones and Two Fannies the Unfortunate Craft.

Unfounded Rumors About the Rochester Freights — Ports and Passages.

CLEVELAND, Aug. 11, — Two schooners were lost Sunday night off Cleveland Harbor. The large three masted schooner Two Fannies went down about twenty miles off shore. The crew of eight kept afloat in the boats until they were picked up by the steamer City of Detroit.

The two masted schooner Fannie L. Jones, heavily loaded with stone from Kelleys Island, went down half a mile from the mouth of the river at 11:45 o'clock Sunday night.

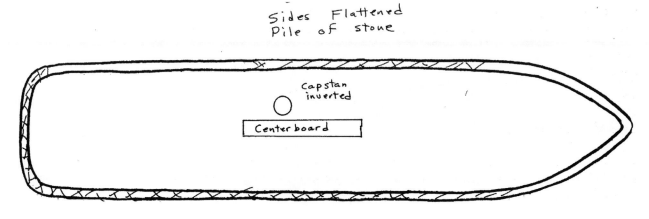

Fannie L. Jones
92'8" x 22'6" x 7'4"
by Georgann S. Wachter
Not to Scale

Jorge B

Official #: 64E419   **Site #:** 61

Location: about ¾ mile east of Pelee Point

Coordinates: LORAN: 43851.2 57184.0   DGPS: 41 56.304 82 29.060

Lies: Bow east   **Depth:** 36 feet

Type: fish tug   **Cargo:** fish and fishing equipment

Power: diesel

Owner(s) Saco Fisheries, Ltd., Adrian Codinha

Built:

Dimensions: approximately 50' x 12'   **Tonnage:** 9 gross

Date of Loss: Friday, September 16, 1983

Cause of Loss: foundered

Jorge B as Miss Julie

Photo courtesy of Frank Prothero, copyright Nan-Sea Publications

Story of the Loss:

The *Jorge B* was first named the *P&E* and her original size was about 40 feet in length.

The *Jorge B* had sailed out of Wheatley, Ontario and was headed for fishing grounds near the Canada/ United States border. This steel turtle back tug foundered suddenly as three lines of thunderstorms passed over the tug. Officials were alerted to the tragedy when a passerby found Joao Paulo Parteira staggering down Pelee National Park's east beach. The seventeen year old and two other young crewmen had swum to shore after their vessel capsized. Parteira's father, Joao Du Parteira, Sr. captained the vessel and went down with the ship. After an intensive search the bodies of Eulidio Fidalgo and Mario Nunes were discovered.

The Portuguese fishing community in the Leamington/Wheatley area was devastated by the loss of three of their community members.

From the Chatham Daily News, September 17, 1983:

Three missing on tug sunk near Point Pelee.

LEAMINGTON, Ont. (CP) — Searchers intensified their efforts today to locate three men missing in Lake Erie since their tug sank Friday near Point Pelee, 65 kilometers southeast of Windsor.

Provential police said the men, whose names were not released, were aboard the 15-metre-long. Georg B, owned by Saco Fisheries, when it suddenly filled with water. They said the crew members were unable to launch a lifeboat.

Police said three other crew members swam to safety and were taken to Leamington District Memorial Hospital, where they were treated for exposure and then released.

The Windsor weather office said three distinct lines of thunderstorms passed over Lake Erie about the time the boat sank.

The Wreck Today:

The wreck's open stern is almost buried while her pilot house still rises from the sand bottom. There are many net floats, gill net and the net reel. Fishnet, poor visibility, and boat traffic are a hazard when diving the *Jorge B*. She is protected from SW winds by Pelee Point.

KEEPSAKE

Official #:	C-80573	**Site #:**	84
Location:	southwest side of Middle Island		
Coordinates:	GPS: position approximate 41°40' 55" 82°41' 15"		
Lies:	scattered	**Depth:**	10 feet
Type:	scow	**Cargo:**	light
Power:	2 masted sail		
Owner(s)	Horace Fleury of Belle River, Ontario		
Built:	1880 in the River Puce, Ontario		
Dimensions:	72'6" x 19'9" x 3'7"	**Tonnage:**	45
Date of Loss:	Friday, August 11, 1911		
Cause of Loss:	ran aground		

Keepsake
Remickk Collection

Story of the Loss:

Fred Oulette, keeper of the Middle Ground Light, and three others had set sail for Sandusky, Ohio to get coal. Sailing in the dark, they drifted off course and ran aground on Gull Island Shoal. The crew from the Marblehead Lifesaving Station took them off the vessel.

Returning to the ship the following day, Oulette and crew were able to pull the *Keepsake* off the shoal and sail her away. Regrettably, the vessel had sustained major damage in the grounding and she was abandoned at nearby Middle Island. Residents of the island stripped the vessel of all items considered to be of any value. Historian Captain Frank E. Hamilton lived on nearby Kelleys Island and is known to have acquired the galley stove and a table.

The Wreck Today

The *Keepsake* lies about 100 feet from the west end of Middle Island and 100 to 150 feet off shore. Wood and hatch covers can be found on the rock bottom among a few remaining mast rings and other metal parts.

DANGER: The waters in this area are very shallow. Approach carefully from the south or east and avoid suffering a similar fate to the *Keepsake* on Gull Island Shoal.

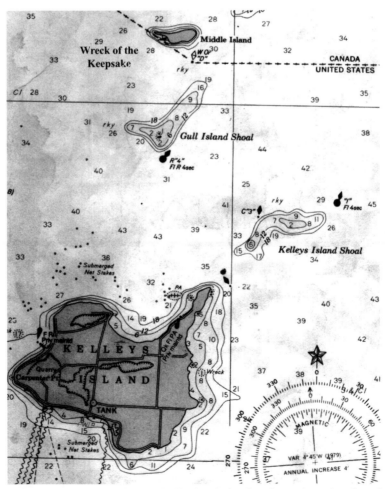

The Keepsake grounded on Gull Island Shoal and was then abandoned on the southwest corner of Middle Island.

L.L. Lamb

Official #: 15609   **Site #:** 6

Location: ¾ mile 338° from Fairport east pierhead light

Coordinates: LORAN: DGPS: PA: 41 46.510 81 17.262

Lies: scattered   **Depth:** 28 feet

Type: schooner   **Cargo:** stone

Power: sail - towed

Owner(s) O. Joslyn *et al*, Donnelly Contracting Company

Built: 1869 in Erie, Pennsylvania by Williams

Dimensions: 120.3 x 26.1 x 10.7   **Tonnage:** 253 gross   240 net

Date of Loss: Saturday, August 16, 1902

Cause of Loss: sprung a leak

L.L. Lamb

C. Patrick Labadie Collection

Story of the Loss:

The *L. L. Lamb* salvaged the engine of the steel-hulled *Algoma* after she struck rock off Mott Island in Lake Superior.

The *L.L. Lamb* was bound from Kelleys Island to Fairport Harbor with a load of stone for the new pier at Fairport. Under tow of the schooner *McCormick*, the *Lamb* sprung a leak about 1½ miles from Fairport. She sank slowly, permitting Captain Dan McClellan and crew to be rescued by the *McCormick*.

On discovering the leak, the vessels signaled for a tug. None made it to her on time. The delay is rumored to have resulted from the fact that the *Lamb* was a union boat and a heated Licensed Tugmen's Protective Association strike was taking place at the time.

The Wreck Today:

The *Lamb* is best located by sounding the large boulders that were her cargo.

Caution: heavy boat traffic.

BOAT SUNK.

The Schooner Lamb Sinks Off Fairport—No Lives Lost.

The schooner Lamb, bound from Kelley's Island to Fairport went to the bottom of Lake Erie at 4:30 o'clock Saturday morning. The Lamb was in tow of the schooner McCormick and both were loaded with stone for the new breakwater. The Lamb sprung a leak about a mile and a half from Fairport Harbor and just abreast of the breakwater. She sank slowly and all of the crew were rescued by the McCormick. The Life Saving crew also went to the rescue but found they were not needed.

Previous to sinking the boats signaled for a tug but none reached them in time although the Annie went out later. It is said that the fact that the Lamb is a union boat had something to do with the delay of the tugs but this can not be substantiated.

Painesville Telegraph -- August 21, 1902

LITTLE WISSAHICKON

Official #:	36351		**Site #:**	21
Location:	28 miles NNE of Avon Point			
Coordinates:	LORAN: 43919.2 57454.7		DGPS: 41 54.217 81 56.781	
Lies:	bow west		**Depth:**	78 feet
Type:	schooner		**Cargo:**	coal
Power:	sail - 3 mast			
Owner(s)	Captain George McKay of Bay City, Michigan			
Built:	1869 at Marine City, Michigan by Rogers			
Dimensions:	148' x 28'		**Tonnage:**	376 gross
Date of Loss:	Friday, July 10, 1896			
Cause of Loss:	sprung a leak			

Wheel of the Little Wissahickon
Photo by Mike Wachter

Story of the Loss:

Through most of her working career, the *Little Wissahickon* was used in the lumber trade.

The *Little Wissahickon* left Buffalo in tow of the Steamer *J.P. Donaldson*. The *Donaldson* also towed the *T.G. Lester*, *A.W. Wright*, and *J.S. Ketchum*. With her four consorts, the *Donaldson* was upbound with coal for Saginaw, Michigan. As they proceed up the stormy lake, the aged *Wissahickon* began to leak worse than usual and her pumps were manned.

Shortly after the crew notified Captain McKay they thought the vessel should be abandoned, two of the crew jumped aboard a raft and two others swam to the *Lester*. The steamer *Tuscarora* rescued the two on the raft six hours later. Captain McKay, cook Mrs. Casey and an unnamed seaman stayed with the vessel and drowned when she finally foundered. It will never be known why they did not take to the yawl boat and save themselves. The surviving crew said that the captain seemed dazed.

The vessel was not insured. According to the newspapers of the time, the lack of insurance indicated that the vessel was not seaworthy.

The Wreck Today:

Ohio divers discovered the Little Wissahickon in 1988. They promptly removed the bell and wrote an article for *Skin Diver* magazine about their find. On reading the article, Canadian authorities were a little upset about the bell snatching (a violation of Canadian law) and demanded its return.

Today, the bell rests at the bow encased in concrete (look for the blob of zebra mussels and scrape them off). On the starboard side there is a lot of chain and one anchor buried in the mud. A second anchor lies on deck on the port side. The wheel can be found knocked over in the hold on the starboard stern. There is considerable fish net around the wreck.

Deadeye and bell of the Little Wissahickon. Note the concrete block encasing the bell.
Photos by Mike Wachter

Little Wissahickon
148' x 28'
by Georgann S. Wachter
Not to Scale

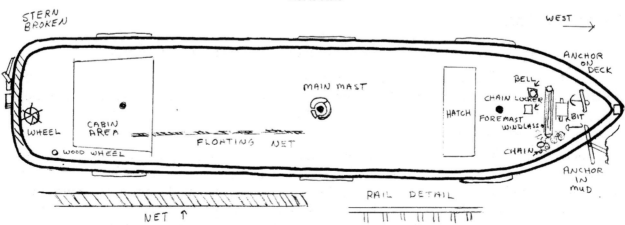

DUKE LUEDTKE

Official #:	216022	**Site #:**	24
Location:	13 miles north of Avon Point, Ohio		
Coordinates:	LORAN: 43825.5 57396.3	DGPS: 41 41.630 81 57.655	
Lies:	bow east	**Depth:**	70 feet
Type:	tug	**Cargo:**	none
Power:	1957 converted to diesel: Original 1890 high pressure non-condensing engine taken from dismantled tug *Townsend Davis*		
Owner(s)	Luedtke Engineering Company, Frankfort, Michigan		
Built:	1917 at Cleveland, Ohio by Great Lakes Towing Company		
Dimensions:	68'7" x 17' x 11'	**Tonnage:**	73 gross 32 net
Date of Loss:	Thursday, September 21, 1993		
Cause of Loss:	sprung a leak		

Duke Luedtke
Great Lakes Historical Society

Story of the Loss:

Named *Alpena* from 1917 to 1974, this tug helped salvage the sunken steamer *Prins Willem V* off Milwaukee Harbor in 1966-67. Luedtke Engineering acquired her from General Piping, Inc. in 1972. She was used with the *Karl D. Luedtke* to move *Derrickboat 16*. Original tonnage 65 gross, 66 net. She was rebuilt in 1957.

The *Duke Luedtke* was en route to Ashtabula, Ohio after transporting dredging equipment from Erie, Pennsylvania to West Harbor, Ohio. Shortly before midnight the crew noticed the tug was moving sluggishly. On checking the engine room, they discovered it filling with water. Mayday calls were made to Coast Guard Stations Lorain and Cleveland. Coast Guard Station Cleveland Harbor responded to the *Luedtke's* call for assistance.

Two Coast Guard seamen, Michael O'Neill and Marvin Thompson, boarded the tug to join Captain Frank Hannan and two crewmen from the tug in a search for the source of the leak. Suddenly, she rolled to port and sank stern first. The crew of the *Luedtke* were thrown in the water and the coastguardsmen were trapped in the sinking tug. Thompson was able to escape by breaking a window with a speaker he tore from the bulkhead and swimming to the surface. Young seaman O'Neil was trapped in the engine room and went down with the tug. The *Luedtke* had been alongside the Coast Guard's 41-foot UTB and the little tug holed the rescue vessel's deck when she plunged to the bottom.

We often forget the heroism of those who go to the aid of mariners in distress. Petty Officer 3rd Class Michael E. O'Neill gave his life rescuing the crew of the Duke Luedtke.

The Wreck Today:

The *Duke Luedtke* lies in 70 feet of water, listing to port in the mud. Her stern is buried. There are tires attached to her sides and hoses scattered around the wreck. The pilothouse door stands open on the port side. This is an easy wreck to penetrate and explore. However, as with all wreck penetration in Lake Erie, she silts up fast. Divers should not enter the wreck without taking necessary wreck penetration precautions.

Round eyed gobies swarm over the wreck of the Duke Luedtke.
Photo by Georgann Wachter

LYCOMING

Official #:	140416	**Site #:**	14
Location:	4 miles east of Rondeau, Ontario		
Coordinates:	LORAN: 44073.0 57566.4	DGPS: 42 15.078 81 53.384	
Lies:	bow north	**Depth:**	26 feet
Type:	propeller	**Cargo:**	coal
Power:	seeple compound engine		
Owner(s)	James O'Conner, Tonawanda, New York		
Built:	1880 at West Bay City, Michigan by Frederick N. Jones (Wheeler Company)		
Dimensions:	251′ x 36′ x 15′3″	**Tonnage:**	1448 gross 1119 net
Date of Loss:	Friday, October 21, 1910		
Cause of Loss:	fire		

Lycoming
Great Lakes Historical Society

Story of the Loss:

The *Lycoming* was built as a sister ship to the *Conemaugh*. Following a fire on board, she was rebuilt as a bulk freighter but retained her hogging arches in 1903.

The *Lycoming* was towing the schooner *Emma C. Hutchinson* upbound from Buffalo, New York to Marquette, Michigan. Captain W. J. Hayes had run the vessels into Rondeau, Ontario to escape a gale on the lake. While in Rondeau Harbor, fire was discovered near her smokestacks about midnight. The westerly gale winds spread the flames quickly and the vessel burned to the water line, sinking in seventeen feet of water. She was later raised and removed to her current location.

The Wreck Today:

Located on a hard pack bottom, the *Lycoming* features a four bladed prop, engine, capstan at the stern, and a large boiler. There is a lot of chain at the bow. Save Ontario Shipwrecks has conducted a survey of this site.

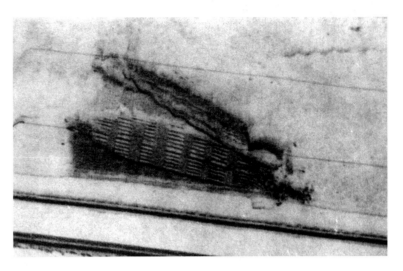

Sidescan image of the wreck of the Lycoming -- courtesy of Roy Pickering.

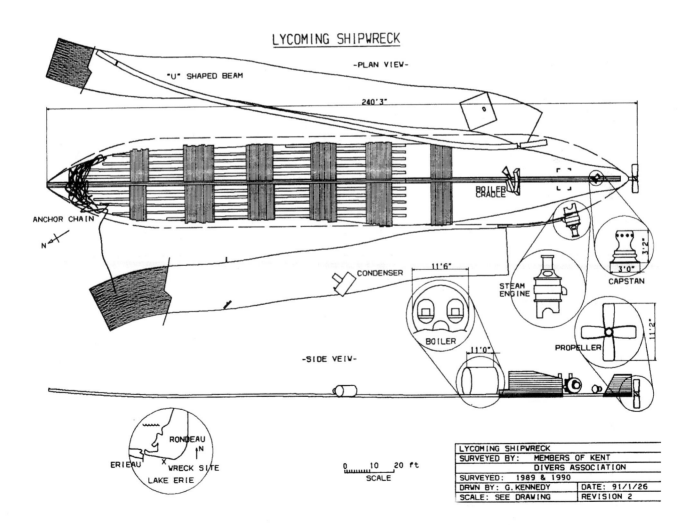

Save Ontario Shipwrecks site survey of the Lycoming conducted by Kent Divers Asssociation 1989-1990.

MAGNET

Official #: 16318   **Site #:** 99

Location: 5.2 miles south 36° 30' west true from Colchester Reef Lighthouse

Coordinates: LORAN: 43757.8 56926.7   DGPS: PA 41 52.87   82 57.40

Lies: scattered   **Depth:** 35 feet

Type: 2 masted schooner   **Cargo:** coal

Power: sail

Owner(s) S. F. Drake of Cleveland, Ohio

Built: 1856 in East Saginaw, Michigan by Malcom Smith in S.R. Kirby yard

Dimensions: 145' x 24'3" x 10'   **Tonnage:** 217.16 gross 206.31 net

Date of Loss: Wednesday, September 12, 1900

Cause of Loss: foundered in storm

Magnet
C. Patrick Labadie Collection

Story of the Loss:

Like many a fine lady, the *Magnet* had a different look for every occasion. She was originally built as a sidewheeler with a vertical beam engine. In 1864, she was rebuilt as a wrecking tug. She was altered to a sloop/barge in 1879 at Detroit. Her final transformation also occurred at Detroit when she was made a schooner in 1888.

Home ported in Harbor Beach, Michigan, and headed for Marine City, Michigan, the *Magnet* was fighting a losing battle with a Lake Erie storm. She was leaking badly and dangerously near sinking when the steamer *Frank E. Kirby* arrived on the scene. The crew of the *Magnet* launched their yawl boat in heavy seas and made for the *Kirby*. As the seas were too rough for the yawl boat to approach the steamer, a line with a life jacket was tossed from the *Kirby*. Mrs. Bennett, the captain's wife, leapt into the sea, grabbed the life jacket, and was hauled aboard the *Kirby*. On several occasions, the stormy seas dashed the yawl boat under the guards of the steamer as the rest of the crew in the small boat were rescued.

Captain Fox of the *Kirby* was commended for his lifesaving efforts.

Lost in this same storm were the schooner *Dundee* and the steamer *John B. Lyon*.

The Wreck Today:

The *Magnet* was cleared as a menace to navigation so her remains are pretty well flattened and scattered.

Marquette & Bessemer No. 2

Official #:	202514	**Site #:**	001
Location:	Six miles off Port Glasgow, on a line from Port Stanley to Erieau, Ontario		
Coordinates:	LORAN: still secret	**DGPS:**	still secret
Lies:	bow west	**Depth:**	70 feet
Type:	steel twin screw car ferry	**Cargo:**	30 rail cars of coal, steel, and castings
Power:	2 triple compound direct acting vertical steam engines, 19+ 31+ 52 x 36 cylinders		
Owner(s)	Marquette & Bessemer Dock and Navigation Company of Conneaut, Ohio		
Built:	1905 at Cleveland, Ohio by American Shipbuilding Company		
Dimensions:	338' x 54' x 19' 6"	**Tonnage:**	2514 gross
Date of Loss:	Wednesday, December 8, 1909		
Cause of Loss:	foundered in storm		

The second Marquette & Bessemer No. 2 at Port Stanley
Port Stanley Train Depot Museum

Story of the Loss:

On December 7, 1909, the four year old car ferry, *Marquette and Bessemer No. 2* left Conneaut, Ohio, bound for Port Stanley, Ontario at 10:40 in the morning. She was loaded with 26 railcars of coal, 3 railcars of steel, and 1 railcar of castings. As the morning passed, she sailed into ferocious weather and was never seen again. Once she left Conneaut, there is much conjecture about where she went and what happened to her, but little that is known to be factual. The storm she sailed into would claim not only the M&B #2, but also the steamers, *Clarion*, *W.C. Richardson*, and two barges. The steamer, *Josiah G. Muir*, would go aground attempting to rescue sailors from the *Clarion*.

Nearly two hours behind schedule, the ferry pulled away from her berth, only to be hailed by a throng of onlookers pointing out that a man had missed the boat. Much to his misfortune, the big ferry reluctantly stopped, and permitted Albert Weiss, treasurer of the Keystone Fish Company of Erie, Pennsylvania, to scurry aboard. Traveling to Port Stanley to consummate the purchase of another company, Mr. Weiss is rumored to have carried $50,000 in his briefcase. As a result, *M&B #2* is considered to be one of Lake Erie's "treasure ships."

Navigating past the harbor light there was no sign of foul weather. Captain Bob McLeod was last seen waving a cheerful farewell to the lighthouse keeper as his vessel entered Lake Erie. The ship could do 12

Marquette & Bessemer No.2 trapped in the ice off Conneaut … Remick Collection

miles an hour in the worst of conditions and the 60 mile trip to Port Stanley was normally no more than a five hour cruise. It is likely that, had she departed on time, she may well have made it safely across the lake.

Many people recounted either seeing or hearing the ill-fated car ferry during the night. Mrs. Adam Large, who lived 10 miles east of Conneaut, said she had seen the car ferry from shore shortly before midnight on Tuesday. She tells of talking about it with her family and then going to look again only to find the lights were gone. At 1:30 in the morning on December 8, ore handler William Rice and his coworkers at Conneaut Harbor, heard distress signals they recognized as coming from the ferry. At about the same time, the master and chief engineer of the steamer, *Black,* claimed to have seen the *Marquette Bessemer No. 2* silhouetted by the Conneaut skyline. At 7:00 a.m. a Canadian from Bruce, Ontario claimed to have heard the car ferry's whistle 7 miles east of Port Stanley. These multiple sightings have led to extensive speculation and much confusion about where the *Marquette & Bessemer No. 2* sank.

Two days after the *Marquette & Bessemer No. 2* sailed, the steamer *William B. Davock,* having survived the gale, sighted wreckage off Long Point on a course for Buffalo. This would prove to be the first confirmed sighting of the *M&B #2.* The following Sunday, the fish tug *Commodore Perry* recovered a ten man lifeboat 15 miles off Erie, Pennsylvania. Partly filled with water, the boat held the bodies of 9 members of the *Marquette & Bessemer No. 2's* crew. None of these men were dressed for the elements.

Captain Bob McLeod

This generated supposition that the car ferry had gone down quickly, leaving no time for her crew to prepare to abandon ship. Four months later, on April 17, 1910, the ice encased body of first mate John McLeod washed into the intake slip of the Niagara Falls Power Plant. It was not until October 7, 1910 that captain Robert McLeod's body was found washed onto the beach on Long Point.

Until the wreck is explored, no one can know what actually happened to the long missing car ferry. One month before she sank, Captain McLeod had complained of almost losing her in a storm as the seas washed over her open stern and flooded her holds. The rising waters had nearly extinguished her boilers. The company had promised to add stern gates to the ship after the season ended. Many speculate that waves rushing over the open stern filled her holds and sunk her. While this may be true, she is known to have been built with 6 watertight bulkheads in her holds. Others speculate that the tie downs on one or more of the rail cars broke loose causing them to roll about the ship in the heavy seas until the *M&B* finally capsized. Still others insist Captain McLeod, knowing his vessel would take water over the stern on rough water, would have headed her into the storm and piloted her toward Erieau, Ontario. Only the 31 folks who died when she went down know for sure.

Compounding her difficulty was the fact that Port Stanley did not have proper navigation lighting. One scenario holds that she made it across the lake only to be unable to enter the harbor safely due to the seas and lack of lighting. If this were the case, she could well have returned to Conneaut to seek safe harbor from the storm. This would explain the reported sightings late in the night. Several petitions for lighting had been submitted to the Canadian government well before the loss of the *Marquette & Bessemer No. 2* but none were acted upon. Following the sinking, Port Stanley established navigation lights, a harbor of refuge, and a lifesaving station.

In a final insult to the ship and her crew, the Marquette & Bessemer Dock and Navigation Company replaced the lost ship with one of very similar design and the exact same name, *Marquette and Bessemer No. 2.* Often the second *M&B #2* is pictured in articles about the lost original. They are best differentiated by their pilothouses. The older boat had an enclosed pilothouse with an open bridge above. As shown on the next page, the new boat had two enclosed pilothouses.

The original Marquette & Bessemer No. 2 was replaced by this vessel, which also carried the name Marquette & Bessemer No. 2
Great Lakes Historical Society

The Wreck Today:

Until very recently, one of the last secrets held by Lake Erie, the *Marquette and Bessemer No. 2* had yet to be found. After she sank, wreckage was found from Port Burwell to Long Point in Canada and from Conneaut past Erie on the US side. Many looked for her without success and, in the summer of 2000, she was finally found.

The crew of the steamer *Black* reported she was headed east when they saw her off Conneaut at 1:30 the morning of the 8th. As a result, most people believed she attempted to return to Conneaut but was unable to enter the harbor. She would have attempted to anchor off Conneaut and ride out the storm until daylight. When her anchors failed to hold, she probably considered making her way to the lee side of Long Point, a 50 mile run in a mountainous following sea. We now know she did not return to Conneaut. Rather, when she could not enter the harbor at Port Stanley, she made a run to the west. The vessel appears to have attempted to make Erieau at the mouth of Rondeau Harbor.

Today a number of her rail cars lay on the lake bottom leading to the wreck of *Marquette & Bessemer No. 2*. She lies in just under 70 feet of water approximately 6 miles off of Port Glasgow, Ontario.

Mecosta

Official #: 91983

Site #: 34

Location: 3 miles north of Bay Village, Ohio

Coordinates: LORAN: 43763.3 57397.3   DGPS: 41 31.850   81 53.001

Lies: bow east

Depth: 50 feet

Type: wood propeller

Cargo: light

Power: triple expansion steam

Owner(s) General Transit Company

Built: 1888 at West Bay City, Michigan by F.W. Wheeler & Company

Dimensions: 281'7" x 40'6" x 20'

Tonnage: 1776.27 gross 1418.32 net

Date of Loss: Sunday, October 29, 1922

Cause of Loss: scuttled

Mecosta

Great Lakes Historical Society

Story of the Loss:

Metal plates were added to the *Mecosta's* hull in a 1919 rebuild. The vessel was used as a model T automobile carrier.

In 1922, the *Mecosta* was stripped of machinery in Lorain, Ohio and towed into the lake by the propeller *Thomas Maytham*. According to accounts, the towline parted in heavy weather and the *Mecosta* anchored. Other accounts say she was scuttled. During the early days of shipwreck hunting, hunters were primarily interested in salvage value and treasure. A letter in our file written to one of these hunters by Captain Frank E. Hamilton — one of the foremost authorities on Great Lakes Shipwrecks — states: "Forget the *Mecosta* she had been up to Lorain getting her boilers and engines out there is nothing in her but the cook's old shoes, I know the fellow that owned her." Based on this tidbit of information, we'd support the theory that she was scuttled.

The Wreck Today:

In April of 1923 the vessel was cleared to a depth of 30 feet. Today she lies in two parts. Shortly after she was discovered, salvers attempting to recover some chain actually turned the vessel over. The wreck has many metal parts strewn about, including a winch. Divers must check out the Victorian bathtub.

The area has heavy boat traffic and most boaters haven't a clue what a dive flag means.

MERIDA

Official #:	92514		**Site #:**	2
Location:	25 miles east of Erieau, Ontario			
Coordinates:	LORAN: 44160.1	57844.0	DGPS:	42 13.955	81 20.788
Lies:	bow southeast		**Depth:**	85 feet
Type:	steel propeller		**Cargo:**	iron ore
Power:	triple expansion steam engine			
Owner(s)	Valley Camp Steamship Company of Cleveland, Ohio			
Built:	1893 by F. W. Wheeler in West Bay City, Michigan			
Dimensions:	360' x 45' x 25'8"		**Tonnage:**	3329 gross 2389 net
Date of Loss:	"Black" Friday, October 20, 1916			
Cause of Loss:	storm			

Merida
Remickk collection

Story of the Loss:

At the time of her launch, in May of 1893, the *Merida* was the largest vessel on the Great Lakes. She also held a record for the biggest cargo. American Steamship Company rebuilt the vessel in 1904. She had a double hull and five watertight bulkheads. These proved insufficient in the wicked waves of Lake Erie.

The *Merida* was downbound from Fort William, Ontario to Buffalo, New York when she ventured into the teeth of the great Lake Erie storm of 1916. The steamer *Frank Billing* followed the *Merida* out of the Detroit River that fateful Friday. However, before reaching the Southeast Shoal, the *Billings* could no longer see the *Merida*. The steamer *Briton* saw her about 12:30 Friday afternoon. At that time she was 25 miles past Southeast Shoal, rolling heavily, and shipping heavy seas over her stern. This was the last sighting.

The *Merida* made another 35 miles before succumbing to the angry lake approximately 60 miles east of Southeast Shoal. Three days after the storm, the steamer *V. D. Mathews* recovered the first three bodies wearing *Merida* life jackets. The fate of Captain Harry Jones and his crew of 23 was no longer in doubt.

A few days after the storm, Port Stanley fish tugs recovered the floating wheelhouse with her brass bell still attached. Not until 60 years later was her exact location pinpointed.

The Wreck Today:

This awesome shipwreck lists slightly to port as she rises from the silty bottom of Lake Erie. Plan on two dives if you want to see the entire wreck. When we first dove her, the entire ship sat above the bottom of the lake. Today, the mid section of the ship disappears into the silt. Most divers dive the stern section first, move the boat to the bow and make their second dive. The stern of the *Merida* is easily penetrated. Caution is required due to heavy silt conditions, depth and the ability to go down more than one deck level. At the bow, you will find heavy damage to her decks and penetration is far more difficult.

A spare propeller blade is on the port side at the stern. Her tiller is hard to port. A capstan and pump are on deck and her engine and boiler can be examined below decks. At the bow is another spare propeller blade, a capstan, and two anchors.

Shipwreck penetration is dangerous. It should only be attempted by divers who are properly trained and equipped for wreck penetration.

The Merida as she appeared before her 1904 rebuild. Note the upper pilot house is open and the aft cabin is further forward. Photo from the Remickk Collection.

F. A. MEYER

Official #: 76731   **Site #:** 22

Location: in shipping lanes 26 miles north of Avon Point

Coordinates: LORAN: 43912.0 57406.4   DGPS: 41 55.439 82 02.953

Lies: bow southwest   **Depth:** 78 feet

Type: wood propeller   **Cargo:** lumber

Power: triple expansion engines

Owner(s) Strong Transportation Company

Built: 1888 by Detroit Dry Dock, Detroit, Michigan

Dimensions: 256'4" x 38'5" x 15'8"   **Tonnage:** 1264 gross 1034 net

Date of Loss: Saturday, December 18, 1909

Cause of Loss: cut by ice

F. A. Meyer as J. Emory Owen
Historical Collections of the Great Lakes

Story of the Loss:

Until 1905 the *Meyer* was named *J. Emory Owen*. In 1903, she burned in the Sturgeon Bay Canal. After being abandoned to underwriters, she was raised and returned to service under her new name.

At the left is the initial report of the loss from the December 20, 1909 Duluth Evening News. Bound for Buffalo from Boyne City, Michigan, the *F.A. Meyer* was cut by ice. The propeller *Mapleton* rescued Captain Charles Kelley and crew.

The Wreck Today:

This shipwreck provides one of the best examples of a wood steamer to be found in Lake Erie. She has five hatches and much of her structure is intact. At the stern, it is possible to penetrate the *Meyer*. Part of her curved rail at the stern has collapsed on the port side. You will also find her capstan in the stern area. The starboard bow is also collapsed. Of interest are her engines and boilers. The boiler gauges are still on the wreck but you'll need to remove some zebra mussels to see them. There is lots of fish net at the bow.

STEAMER MEYERS SUNK BY THE ICE

Another Boat Goes Down in Lake Erie---Crew Saved By Mapleton.

St. Catherines, Ont., Dec. 20.—Ice cutting through the hull of the steamer F. A. Meyers of Tonawanda, caused her to sink, twenty-five miles off Port Colborne, in Lake Erie, yesterday afternoon. The crew of eighteen were taken off by the steamer Mapleton. The Meyers was from Boyne City to Buffalo, with a cargo of lumber.

**Duluth Evening Herald
December 20, 1909**

F. A. Meyer as J. Emory Owen with her her tows, Michigan &Elizabeth A. Nicholson at Hubbard Woods. Illinois
Historical Collections of the Great Lakes

PHILIP MINCH

Official #: 150427   **Site #:** 68

Location: 8 miles east of Middle Island

Coordinates: LORAN: 43741.9 57106.2   DGPS: 41 41.304 82 30.808

Lies: bow northeast   **Depth:** 47 feet

Type: propeller   **Cargo:** light

Power: three cylinder steeple compound steam engine with two scotch boilers

Owner(s) Nicholas Transit Company, manager William Gerlach of Cleveland, Ohio

Built: 1888 at Cleveland, Ohio by William Radcliffe

Dimensions: 275' x 40'8" x 22'   **Tonnage:** 2010 gross 1657 net

Date of Loss: Sunday, November 20, 1904

Cause of Loss: fire

Philip Minch
Historical Collections of the Great Lakes

Story of the Loss:

A fire of undetermined origin started in the stern of the *Minch* as she was traveling light from Conneaut to Sandusky, Ohio for a load of coal. Captain Benson and crew fought the fire for two hours before he woke the rest of his crew and ordered them to the lifeboats. Meanwhile a Marblehead Light Station crew under command of Captain Grieser started for the burning vessel. The lifesaving crew spent the night looking for the shipwrecked crew of the *Minch*, not knowing they had landed, cold but safe, in Sandusky.

From the *Detroit Free Press*, November 21, 1904:

Driven Off By Flames

The wooden steamer Philip Minch, managed by William Gerlach of Cleveland, burned to the water's edge in Lake Erie eight miles east of Marblehead at midnight Saturday night and the entire crew, consisting of seventeen men, were forced to quit the ship. The fire started in the stern of the ship from some cause as yet not ascertained. So rapidly did the flames spread that several members of the crew, asleep in their bunks, did not have time to dress and escaped to the deck clad only in their underclothes and leaving all their personal effects behind. No effort was made to extinguish the flames after the arrival of the lifesavers, as the ship was afire from stem to stern and further efforts toward extinguishing the fire would simply have been a needless and hopeless risk of life.

From the *Toledo Blade*, November 21, 1904:

Marine News

Burned to the Water's Edge

All night on Lake Erie in a rowboat, looking for shipwrecked sailors who were not there, was the experience of the Marblehead lifesaving crew Saturday night and Sunday morning. Shortly before midnight Saturday the lookout at the station saw a vessel on fire, about 12 miles east of Marblehead. The crew was at once routed out and the boats manned. As swiftly as possible they pulled to the burning vessel, which was practically destroyed before the life savers could reach it. The search for the crew began at once. In ever widening circles the boats scoured the lake, looking in vain for men or corpses. Not until 7 o'clock Sunday morning was the search abandoned. Immediately upon arriving at the station Captain Grieser, who is in charge, telephoned to the city and learned that the crew of the burned vessel had escaped in boats and rowed to this port, arriving here shortly before 1 o'clock. The crew and lifesavers must have passed within a very short distance of each other near the mouth of the Sandusky Bay.

The Wreck Today:

The engine of the *Minch* was surprisingly intact, although the rest of the vessel burned to the waterline. Until 1996, the engine stood upright. An ore boat hit it in 1996 and knocked it askew. There is a huge boiler and firebox covered with lots of zebra mussels. Starboard of the stern is a capstan and her winch sits on the port bow. This wreck is wrapped in gill nets and, while local divers have tied down most, caution is necessary to avoid becoming entangled in the nets.

Side scan image of the Philip Minch courtesy of Aqua Vision Research.

MORNING STAR

Official #:   **Site #:**   50

Location: 8 miles north of Lorain, Ohio
Coordinates: LORAN: 43752.7 57246.6   DGPS: 41 36.813   82 12.531
Lies: bow south   **Depth:** 65 feet
Type: sidewheel steamer   **Cargo:** passengers, mowing machines, pig iron,
                                                   boxes of glass and cheese, stone, oil, etc.
Power: vertical beam engine; 60.5" x 11' stroke cylinder;   38' sidewheels; Machinery built
                   for the *Ocean* by T.F. Secor of New York, New York
Owner(s)   Detroit and Cleveland Steam Navigation Company, Detroit, Michigan
Built: 1862 at Trenton, Michigan by Alvin A. Turner; Launched June 7, 1862
Dimensions: 243' x 34' x 14'   **Tonnage:**   1,141
Date of Loss: Saturday, June 20, 1868
Cause of Loss: collision with the bark Cortland

Morning Star
Collection of Ralph Roberts

Story of the Loss:

The *Morning Star* made her first run August 31, 1862 from Detroit to Cleveland. She carried the 20th
Regiment Michigan Volunteers to join the Federal Armies. Her entire career was spent on the Detroit to

Cleveland run. She was subject to arson on November 20, 1866 when a Detroit rogue over insured a shipment of merchandise planning to set the ship afire on its Cleveland run. Not wanting to risk his own life, the swindler hired an incompetent arsonist that was foiled by an alert crew. For her entire life, she was plagued with minor mechanical problems including a fractured walking beam on November 25, 1866 and a cracked piston head in May of 1868. On both of these occasions she was towed to Detroit by her sister ship the *R.N. Rice*.

Bound from Cleveland to Detroit with 38 passengers and a number of immigrants, the *Star's* departure had been delayed while loading approximately 20 tons of pig iron. Having sat out an intermittent rain while loading, she sailed into a dark night and a moderate sea. The bark *Cortland*, bound from Sheboygan, Michigan to Cleveland approached from the opposite direction. The *Cortland's* mate had removed her green light to clean and trim it. As he replaced it, the two vessels collided. Twenty feet of the *Morning Star's* bow was ripped off, and the *Cortland* was hauled beneath the steamer's guards into the paddle wheels. Both vessels went to the bottom 15 miles NE of Vermilion Ohio. All but two of the *Cortland's* crew survived. Some 36 of the 90 passengers and crew aboard the *Morning Star* perished. Fourteen were saved from the Morning Star after taking refuge on the hurricane deck which had torn loose. The *R.N. Rice*, sister ship of the *Morning Star*, picked up the survivors.

The Wreck Today:

On July 28, 1868, the tug *SS Coe* recovered 2 anchors and 45 fathoms of chain. In September of 1868 a salvage attempt was made and the *Morning Star* was moved about 10 miles from the spot she sank. Today, she sits upright in 60 to 70 feet of water 8 miles north of Lorain Harbor. The huge boiler rises 30 feet from the bottom and her walking arm and lower portions of the paddle wheels are reasonably intact. The decks are collapsed and the mowing machines that once could be seen off her starboard side have been covered with silt or moved.

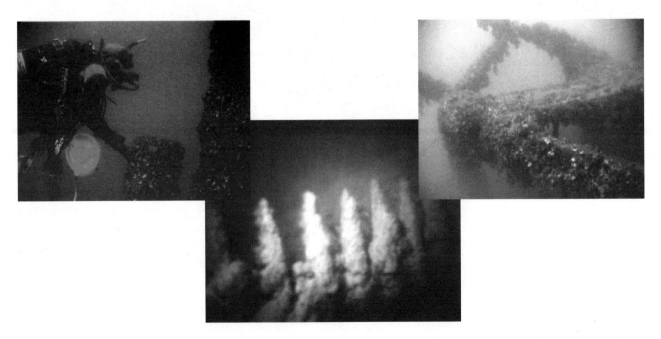

Georgann examines the boiler stack, mowing machine, walking beam on the wreck of the Morning Star
Photos by Mike Wachter

Morpeth Schooner (Phalarope?)

Official #:   **Site #:**   13

Location: 1/4 mile from shore off Morpeth, Ontario

Coordinates: LORAN: 44133.0   57629.1   DGPS: 42 22.443   81 49.275

Lies: bow southwest   **Depth:**   14

Type: 3 mast   **Cargo:**   stone

Power: sail

Owner(s)

Built:

Dimensions: approximately 123' x 24'   **Tonnage:**   approximately 300

Date of Loss:

Cause of Loss: driven aground

Mainmast Step on Morpeth Schooner
Georgann Wachter

Story of the Loss:

The identity of this vessel is still unknown. Our best guess is that she is the schooner *Phalarope* official # 19766. The *Phalarope* came ashore near Rondeau, Ontario during a storm on September 29, 1872. She was built in 1854 at Cleveland, Ohio by Rodney Caulkins. The boat underwent a rebuild in 1869. She measured 136' x 25' x 11' and was 371 gross ton. At the time of her loss she was owned in Milwaukee. The schooner *Courtlandt* went ashore in the same area during this storm and was also abandoned.

From the Detroit Free Press, October 10, 1872:

>   Two Vessels Abandoned. — The wreckers, which left several days since to rescue the schooner Phalarope, ashore near the Eau, on Lake Erie, failed in the undertaking and have returned. The vessel has been abandoned, and doubtless will be suffered to go to pieces unless others renew the attempt. The vessel was eighteen years old and was built at Cleveland by Rodney Calkins. She was 371 tons burden, and was owned at Milwaukee. The party which visited the same locality to rescue the schooner Courtlandt have

also abandoned that vessel. She has become badly broken up, so much so that steam pumps bad no effect on her whatever. She too was an old vessel, having been twenty-four years in commission. She was built at Cleveland by Seth C. Degroat, and for a few years was brig rigged subsequently to a fore-and-after. She was 234 tons, old style, and for several years has hailed from Detroit. Both the above are being stripped of their outfit.

The Wreck Today

Located on a sand bottom, the *Morpeth Schooner* can be shore dove (with permission) off the stairway of a nearby green house. Unusual features of her construction are the iron hanging knees used to support her deck and masts. On most schooners, these would be made of wood. The "L" shaped knees are 4" wide and 2" thick.

Algae and fish are abundant in the summer months. The vessel is filled with stone and wood debris. In the summer of 2000, attempts by Canadian divers to locate the wreck were unsuccessful. With the lower lake levels, she may have silted over.

Bow chains, metal support, and bow stem of the Morpeth Schooner
Photos by Georgann Wachter

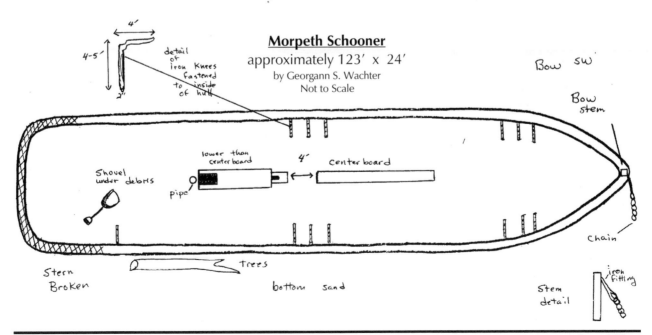

Amaretta Mosher

Official #: 389   **Site #:** 91

Location: Starve Island Reef, WSW from 7 foot mark on chart to 15 feet

Coordinates: PA: 41 36.79   82 48.86

Lies: bow southwest, scattered   **Depth:** 25 feet

Type: schooner   **Cargo:** coal

Power: sail, 3 masts

Owner(s) J.M. Shacket of Marine City & Captain David Hutchinson of Port Huron

Built: 1867 in Ashtabula, Ohio by Gershom A. Thayer

Dimensions: 134'9" x 24'8" x 10'9"   **Tonnage:** 300.91 gross 285.87 net

Date of Loss: Saturday, November 23, 1902

Cause of Loss: storm

Amaretta Mosher

University of Detroit Mercy Archives, Fr. Edward Dowling Collection

Story of the Loss:

The rigging of the *Amaretta Mosher* was changed from two masts to three masts in 1885. After her rebuild, she was fined $30.00 for not having her tonnage carved on her main beam.

The steam barge *D.F. Rose* was towing the *Mosher*, *Wawanash*, and *Lyman Casey* when she encountered heavy weather. The *Amaretta Mosher* stranded on Starve Island Reef and the *D. F. Rose* was beached on South Bass Island after being damaged on the reef. The other tows proceeded to Port Huron. This late fall storm also claimed the steamer *Quito* at Lorain, Ohio.

A series of entries in the 1902 Annual Report of the Chief of Engineers tell the tale after her loss:

> The schooner *Mosher* was wrecked on Starve Island Reef (examined and found not to be a hazard to navigation).

> This vessel ran on Starve Island Reef November 30 (1902) and became a total wreck sliding off into deeper water and going to pieces. Its location was determined but owing to the lateness of the season no steps could be taken toward its removal until spring when the elements had so disposed of it that there remained no danger to navigation.

> About the end of November 1902 it was reported that the two masted schooner *Amerette Mosher* was ashore and wrecked on Starve Island Reef. This vessel of 300 gross tonnage was built in 1867. It was visited on December 1 by U.S. Inspection Boat found to be abandoned and in a position where it was not an obstruction to navigation and where it was liable to slip off into deep water. The wreck was visited from time to time, in the spring of 1903 some portion of it still visible. An arrangement was made to break it up or remove it making use of the United States dredge then bound from Toledo to Huron. When the dredge arrived however on May 13 nothing could be found of the wreck. It had apparently been completely broken up and on examination, revealed no portion of it and it is thought that it is no longer an obstruction to navigation.

The Wreck Today:

The *Mosher* lies badly broken and scattered on rock bottom. There is a great deal of boat traffic in this area.

MOUNT VERNON

Official #:   **Site #:**   63

Location: 3 miles south of Point Pelee

Coordinates: sorry, still secret

Lies: east/west, broken and scattered   **Depth:** 25 feet

Type: wood propeller   **Cargo:** corn, flour, wheat

Power: steam engine

Owner(s) Western Transportation Company, Buffalo, New York

Built: 1854 by F. D. Ketchum and Keating, Huron, Ohio

Dimensions: 178′ x 29′4″ x 11′8″   **Tonnage:** 577

Date of Loss: Tuesday, October 9, 1860

Cause of Loss: explosion

Mineral Rock, similar to the Mount Vernon
Eric Heyl

Story of the Loss:

While en route from Detroit to Buffalo the *Mount Vernon* was delayed a day by heavy weather in Pigeon Bay. Shortly after Captain Newman got the vessel under way, and while abreast of Point Pelee, she exploded. In addition to injuring several other people, the explosion killed the second engineer and a fireman. Although she sank in twenty minutes, the remaining crew (about 20 people) were able to climb her mast and upper works. Several vessels picked the crew up at day break and took them to Detroit.

The story is well told in the following article from the Thursday, October 11, 1860 *Cleveland Plain Dealer*:

Loss of the Mount Vernon.

The Detroit papers contain particulars of the propeller *Mount Vernon*. The propeller left Detroit for Buffalo on Sunday evening with a cargo consisting of 19,200 bushels of corn, 488 barrels flour, and 150 bags wheat. Before leaving the river she encountered a heavy gale and was compelled to lie by at Malden all night. Left Monday morning 20 minutes to 4, and ran down six miles below Point au Pelee, the wind blowing fresh from NE, with heavy sea. The storm increasing in violence, run back for shelter in Pigeon Bay under the Point, from whence she again got under way at 1 o'clock that morning. When 1/4 of a mile from the "Dummy," off Point an Pelee, Capt. Newman observing that she was going very slow, went aft to see what steam was on. Looked down from the Upper deck and ascertained that she had on 50 pounds, (being capable of carrying 70 pounds.) Went back to the man at the wheel and ordered him to put the wheel starboard and keep her ESE. Just as he had spoken the boiler blew up with a terrific explosion, tearing away her after part entire, breaking off both arches, and blowing away the after part of the cabin.

Theodore Reese 2d engineer, and James Conklin fireman were scalded so badly as to render their death instantaneous. Reese was about 24 years of age, and leaves a wife in Buffalo. Conklin was about 22 years of age, and unmarried.

Capt. Newman got upon the top of the pilothouse to look after the boats, and found them both blown away. A very few minutes afterwards, the steamer fell over on her beam ends. When she fell, Capt. Newman was in the office to look after the money. The stove and lounge fell on him, but he had previously taken the precaution to secure a line from the mast, and made his escape. The wreck soon after went down tearing the cabin and upper deck, from which a raft was soon constructed, fastened together with a rope cut from the square sail, but fortunately the crew were not reduced to the necessity of resorting to such frail means of preservation. After clinging to the rigging till daylight, the surviving crew, 20 in number, were taken off by Capt. Mobley of the schooner Lookout, bound for Buffalo. Capt. Howard, of the schooner Fax also came alongside and proffered assistance, but it was not needed. Soon after steamer Ocean Capt. Evans, Came along, and took the crew on board and carried them to Detroit.

The *Mt. Vernon* was a stanch propeller of 57 tons, and came out in 1856. She is understood to be insured for about $15,000. The cargo was shipped by J. L. Hurd & Co., of Detroit and was fully insured. The cause of the explosion is unknown.

The story of the *Mount Vernon* was not to end with her sinking and the loss of two lives. A short time after the *Mount Vernon* was lost, the *Zadock Pratt* struck the sunken *Mount Vernon* and was lost.

The Wreck Today:

The *Mount Vernon* lies scattered in 25 feet of water. Her keelson and lower hull members are flat on the bottom and some small machinery, windlass, blocks, turnbuckle, and a pump lie to the south of this structure. Immediatly to the east of the wreck lie the remains of the *Zadock Pratt*. The bottom is sandy and there are many small fish and fresh water sponges.

PADDY MURPHY

Official #: 150271   **Site #:** 37

Location: ¼ mile off Bay Village, Ohio

Coordinates: LORAN: 43737.6 57357.8   DGPS: 41 30.296 81 56.377

Lies: bow southeast   **Depth:** 10 feet

Type: tug   **Cargo:** towed schooner *Republic*

Power: steam

Owner(s) Thomas Maythem of Buffalo

Built: 1882 by John Babtiste Martel at Saugatuck, Michigan

Dimensions: 68'8" x 17'4" x 8'9"   **Tonnage:** 42.21 gross 21.21 net

Date of Loss: Monday, April 23, 1888

Cause of Loss: fire

Story of the Loss:

The *Paddy Murphy* first entered the water in mid September of 1882. She was painted green with a red stripe and named in honor of one of her owners, Patrick Murphy of Chicago.

While towing the schooner *Republic*, the *Murphy* caught fire, was run aground, and burned to the water's edge. The crew escaped without injury. Thomas Axworthy had recently sold the *Paddy Murphy*, but ice at Buffalo prevented her delivery.

The Wreck Today:

Located on a sand bottom, there is a large propeller and shaft, pipes, and a small boiler. A large tree lies along the port side. As the wreck is just west of Huntington Beach State Park, there is a lot of boat traffic.

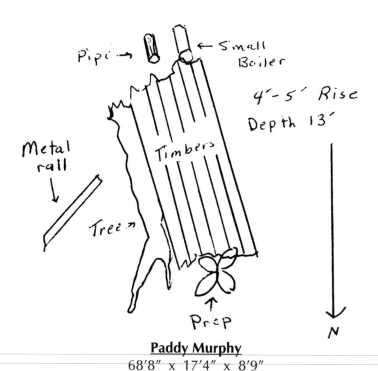

Paddy Murphy
68'8" x 17'4" x 8'9"
by Georgann S. Wachter
Not to Scale

NET WRECK

Official #:   **Site #:**   57

Location: 14 miles east of Point Pelee

Coordinates: LORAN: 43889.2   57307.6   DGPS: 41 56.564   82 14.872

Lies: bow west   **Depth:**   70 feet

Type: schooner   **Cargo:**   coal

Power: sail

Owner(s)

Built:

Dimensions: approximately 90' x 18'   **Tonnage:**

Date of Loss:

Cause of Loss:

Story of the Loss:

Unknown.

The Wreck Today:

This unknown wreck sits upright on a mud bottom. She has pumps, winch, deadeyes, an L shaped shovel, wood blocks, windlass, and anchor. Old hemp fishnet wraps the wreck.

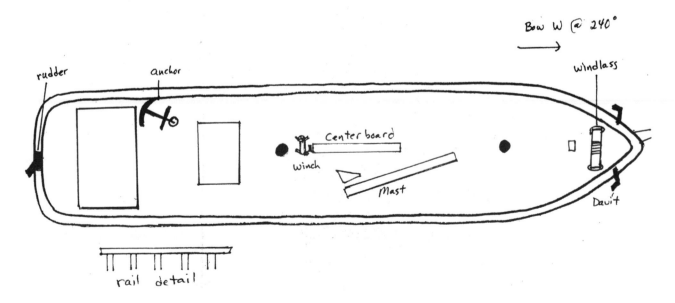

Net Wreck
90' x 18'
by Georgann S. Wachter
Not to Scale

NEW BRUNSWICK

Official #:   **Site #:**   59

Location: 4 miles south of Port Alma, Ontario

Coordinates: LORAN: 43950.9   57321.2   DGPS: 42 06.776   82 18.117

Lies: bow west   **Depth:** 53 feet

Type: bark   **Cargo:** white oak and black walnut timbers

Power: sail

Owner(s)   Henry Eberts, Chatham, Ontario

Built: 1847 at St. Catherines, Ontario by Louis Shikluna

Dimensions: 128'8" x 22'   **Tonnage:**   296

Date of Loss: Thursday, August 26, 1858

Cause of Loss: lost rudder in gale and rolled

New Brunswick
drawing from Toronto Star, August 19, 1939

Story of the Loss:

In 1847, this ship made the first shipment of grain to Europe from the Great Lakes. Margaret Goodman, possibly the only woman diver in the country in 1922, was hired to salvage the *New Brunswick*. She failed to locate the vessel. Miss Goodman had gained fame for her successful salvage of copper off the *Pewabic* in 1916. Other salvage attempts followed including one by Miss Goodman without "reported" success. In 1980, diver Mike Dilts relocated the wreck. His team did extensive survey work and recovered artifacts and oak timbers. However, no black walnut remained to be found.

On August 25, 1858, Captain Angus McTavish and crew left Lake St. Clair with a load of walnut and oak timbers stacked high on the decks of the *New Brunswick*. Her final destination was supposed to be

Montreal, but the tempests of the lake dictated otherwise. A gale out of the south-southwest struck the vessel causing the rudder to fail. Caught in the troughs of the waves, the vessel went over on her side, the deck cargo tearing the ship apart. As she settled to the bottom, the crew climbed to the crosstrees. Four men drowned by morning. Captain McTavish and the remaining crew fashioned a raft and paddled toward shore. One more crewman perished before the captain and three others were rescued by 5 men in a rowboat that leaked so badly everyone on board had to bail water to keep it afloat.

From The *Detroit News,* October 11, 1934:

MRS. GOODMAN has contract to recover lumber on ship lost in 1859. - Mrs. Margaret Campbell Goodman, of Brooklyn, New York, known since 1917 as the only woman deep-sea diver in the country, said today that she has contracted to raise the cargo of logs, worth many thousand dollars, which was lost in Lake Erie, four miles off Point Pelee, when the schooner *New Brunswick* sank in 1859.

"I am more than 60 years old now and I won't do any of the recovery work myself but I will go under water at least once to look over the site," Mrs. Goodman said. She is in Detroit on business in connection with her venture.

"Because I am the only woman diver in the country all my dives have been exaggerated. This ship is in only about 40 feet of water and it should not be especially difficult, once we locate it. But I am not as young as I used to be and my work will be principally in directing operations."

Mrs. Goodman first will view the scene of the salvaging operations from an airplane.

"I will fly over the approximate location with a photographer," she explained. "From a high altitude we should be able to see the wreck. If we can't see it with our eyes maybe the camera plates will catch it.

"If we have good luck we should locate the wreck and have the cargo on our barge within two weeks. The weather may turn bad on us, however."

Mrs. Goodman's most noted feat was the salvaging in 1917, of $300,000 worth of copper from the *Pewabic* which had been lying at the bottom of Lake Huron since 1865 and had defied five previous salvaging attempts.

Mrs. Goodman considered trying to salvage the *New Brunswick* in 1920.

The Wreck Today:

Due to the extensive salvage operations, the wreck is pretty well flattened. The centerboard is standing. There is a mast on the starboard side and a rail with deadeyes on the starboard stern. She sits on a hard pack bottom.

This side scan image was taken by Jim Kennard when he found the New Brunswick on May 4, 1980.
Remickk Collection

Isaac W. Nicholas

Official #: 13477   **Site #:** 77

Location: Grubb's Reef

Coordinates: LORAN: 43819.4   57138.7   DGPS: 41 52.934 82 32.695

Lies: bow west   **Depth:** 36 feet

Type: schooner, three masted   **Cargo:** ore

Power: sail

Owner(s) Phillip Minch of Vermillion, Ohio

Built: 1862 at Vermillion, Ohio by Isaac W. Nicholas

Dimensions: 137.8′ x 26.2′ x 12.2′   **Tonnage:** 318

Date of Loss: Monday, October 20, 1873

Cause of Loss: storm

R.P. Mason similar to the Isaac W. Nicholas

Remickk Collection

Story of the Loss:

The *Nicholas* was downbound from Escanaba, Michigan en route to Cleveland, Ohio when she came upon the violent waves of a fierce storm. Captain H. L. Foster encountered such heavy seas when he reached Point Pelee that he chose to guide his vessel back into Pigeon Bay for shelter. Setting anchor in company of several other vessels, the *Nicholas* was prepared to wait out the storm.

Several hours later, the tempest came around from another direction with even greater fury than before. Against the violence of the waves, the vessel dragged her anchors until she was pounding bottom on an uncharted reef. She continued to pound on the rocks until she sank. Compelled to climb the rigging for their continued safety, the crew clung to the masts through the night. The following morning, the Canadian schooner *Denmark* sent a yawl boat to their rescue. After the rescue, the crew was transferred to the tug *Champion* and carried safely to Detroit.

Grubb Reef

Nineteen years later, W.A. Grubb, light keeper at Point Pelee filed a report the existence of a shoal about three miles WNW of the light station dummy. He described the shoal as having two shallow spots, one composed of stone and boulders and the other made up of a wreck, probably that of the *I.W. Nicholas*. He had noted that some ice remained near the shoal after all other ice had disappeared and he established ranges on shore to assist in a future survey. The following season a hydrographic survey team charted the shoal and the wreck. In their report they state:

> Had it not been for the ranges established by Captain Grubb it is doubtful if the party would have discovered the shoal in this locality. It certainly would not have done so without a great loss of time. It is important that as dangerous a shoal as this, so close to the track of vessels, should have a name so that it would quickly catch the eye of anyone using the chart. Captain Grubb's assistance having been entirely voluntary and having been of great use to the survey, I have therefore to suggest the name of Grubb Reef for the two shoals at this point.

From that day forward the twin shoals on which the *I.W. Nicholas* lies have been shown on the charts as "Grubb Reef".

The Wreck Today:

This excellent wreck lies on a sand and silt bottom. There is a wheel, rudder, and steering gear. A couple of wood blocks lay on the wreck as well as deadeyes and belaying pins. The windlass is to starboard and the anchor is on the wreck. A metal spoked wheel at the bow may have been part of a winch.

Watch for heavy boat traffic and snagged nets.

NORTH CAROLINA

Official #:	205129	**Site #:**	8
Location:	¾ mile off Mentor-on-the-Lake, Ohio		
Coordinates:	LORAN: 43934.3 57709.3	DGPS: 41 43.808 81 22.885	
Lies:	Bow south	**Depth:**	40 feet
Type:	tug	**Cargo:**	light
Power:	diesel		
Owner(s)	Great Lakes Towing Company, Cleveland, Ohio		
Built:	1908 at Chicago by Dunham Towing & Wrecking Company (Great Lakes Towing)		
Dimensions:	74'8" x 19'9" x 11'6"	**Tonnage:**	97 gross 66 net
Date of Loss:	Monday, December 9, 1968		
Cause of Loss:	foundered		

North Carolina
Great Lakes Historical Society

Story of the Loss:

She was named *L.C. Sabin* until 1941. As the *Sabin,* she was stationed at the Soo for years and helped many vessels transiting the locks. She was converted to diesel in 1951. This is the first shipwreck the authors ever dove.

Captain Steven Horvath and his crew had driven to Cleveland from Conneaut, Ohio to board the *North Carolina*. They were heading back toward Conneaut when they discovered the stern was low in the water. Soon, they lost all electrical power and were unable to radio for help or to run the pumps.

Fortunately, Mrs. Herman Black, who lived along the lake, had notified the Coast Guard that a tug was offshore and not moving. Coast Guard vessels from Cleveland, Fairport, and a chopper from Detroit were dispatched. Meanwhile, Captain Horvath, engineer Albert Kettell and crewmen Eino Salo boarded a small fiberglass lifeboat and pulled for shore. Around 3:00 p.m., before help arrived, the *North Carolina* went to the bottom. The captain believed water was pouring in through the rudder cable holes.

From the December 10, 1968 *Cleveland Plain Dealer*:

LAKE CLAIMS TUG;

3 ABOARD SAVED

Coast Guard equipment converged from all parts of Lake Erie yesterday afternoon to rescue a three-man tugboat crew and make a futile attempt to save the boat. The 81-foot North Carolina property of Great Lakes Towing Co., went down in 32 feet of choppy water at a point 1½ to two miles north; of Mentor-on-the-Lake and five miles west of Fairport Harbor. The crew was picked up by a 40-foot boat from the Coast Guard's Fairport Harbor Station. It was summoned by Mentor-on-the-Lake police, who noticed the North Carolina's stern settling low in the water. Rescued were Capt. Stephen Horvath, 40, of 849 Harbor Avenue, Conneaut; engineer Albert Kettell, 64, of 996 Buffalo Street, Conneaut, and Eino Salo of Erie, Pa.

The tug was en route to Buffalo from the Great Lakes dock in Cleveland. A stop and crew change in Conneaut were planned. Cause of the sinking is not known. The engine room began flooding about noon. Electrical equipment, including pumps and the radio, apparently was put out of action immediately. In addition to the Fairport Harbor boat, the Coast Guard, sent two boats with salvage pumps from Cleveland, a buoy tender from Cleveland, a pump-equipped helicopter from Detroit. But, the tug was already gone. The Coast Guard also received a call from Mrs. Herman Black, 7563 Salida Road, Mentor-on-the-Lake, who watched from her lakefront home as the North Carolina slowed, stopped and began to sink.

The Wreck Today:

The tug lays upright w
port on a sand and ro
bottom. Ice has cause
wheelhouse to collaps
The stack, boiler, and
wheelhouse roof lay c
the wreck on the port
side. You can also
explore her cast steel
bladed prop and large
rudder.

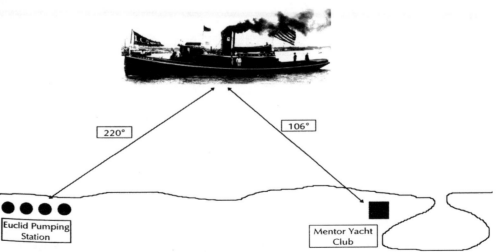

Shore sightings for the North Carolina.

NORTHERN INDIANA

Official #:

Site #:   74

Location: just west of Point Pelee, Ontario

Coordinates: LORAN: 43830.7   57160.4   DGPS: 41 53.882   82 30.600

Lies: bow east   **Depth:**   25 feet

Type: paddle wheel steamer   **Cargo:**   passengers & misc. freight

Power: verticle beam engine - 72" x 12' stroke with 38' paddle wheels

Owner(s)   Michigan Southern Railroad Company

Built: 1852 at Buffalo, New York by Bidwell & Banta

Dimensions: 300'6" x 36'10" x 13'8"   **Tonnage:**   1,475

Date of Loss: Thursday, July 17, 1856

Cause of Loss: fire

Northern Indiana
Great Lakes Historical Society

Story of the Loss:

Along with her sister ship, *Southern Michigan*, the *Northern Indiana* was built for the Michigan and Southern Railroad Company's passenger service between Buffalo, New York and Toledo, Ohio. Both vessels were elaborately equipped to appeal to passengers. However, the *Northern Indiana* became known as the "hard luck sister" due to a series of incidents in her maiden year, 1852. She rammed the schooner *Plymouth* 35 miles west of Cleveland, Ohio on June 23. The *Plymouth* and her cargo of

10,000 bushels of wheat rapidly sank. During a September 21, gale both her arches were broken off as the waves twisted and tore at the ship. Her machinery failed and she was at the mercy of the seas for over five hours before repairs could be made and she was able to slowly make Toledo, Ohio.

Hard luck sailed with her on her final voyage as well. When one would least expect disaster, on calm seas in the midst of a balmy July day, fire broke out in the engine room of the *Northern Indiana*. With her master, Captain Phett, lying ill in Buffalo, she was sailing under command of the first mate. As soon as the fire was noted, first mate W.H. Wetmore rang bell signals to stop the engine. The fire was spreading so rapidly that the crew was forced to abandon the engines before obeying the acting captain.

The steamer *Mississippi* and the propeller *Republic* were some five miles astern of the flaming boat. A schooner was also near by. The unattended engine drove the stricken passenger ship rapidly away from the schooner and the fires were fanned and driven aft. As the blazing vessel steamed out of control, steamers *Mississippi* and *Republic* converged on her. The crew fashioned makeshift life preservers from planking and lines off the hurricane deck and, as the flames drove them away, cut the forward deck to pieces for additional floats. Many passengers leapt to the water and grabbed for their lives at this floating debris.

When the rising water finally stopped the *Northern Indiana's* engines, the *Mississippi* and *Republic* were able to save about 100 people; the loss of life was reported to be as high as 56 people (later, more reliable reports state 28 lost their lives). Standing true to tradition, acting captain, Mate W.H. Wetmore, was last to leave the stricken sidewheeler.

The Wreck Today:

Lying on a sand bottom, the most notable feature of the wreck is her boiler. The wreck is broken and spread over a large area. There is lots of pipe and wood, a second small boiler, and a capstan. If you search carefully, you may find one of the brass tags labeled "M.S. & N.I.R.R. The initials stand for Michigan Southern and Northern Indiana Rail Road. They helped to positively identify this site as the *Northern Indiana*

CAUTION: This vessel lies very close to the Pelee Point shoal waters. Boaters need to pay careful attention to the depth to the east of the wreck. The area is also subject to very strong currents and divers need to exercise great caution in the water.

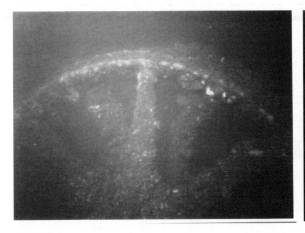 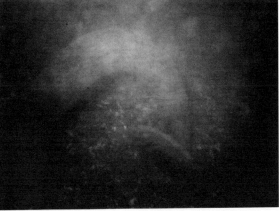

The wreck of the Northern Indiana is littered with many metal engine parts
Photos by Georgann Wachter

OLIVE BRANCH

Official #:   **Site #:**   7

Location: just east of the mouth of the Grand River, Fairport, Ohio

Coordinates: LORAN: DGPS: 41 45.697   81 16.557

Lies: buried and scattered   **Depth:**   6 feet

Type: sloop   **Cargo:**   general merchandise

Power: sail

Owner(s)

Built: 1816 at Henderson Harbor, New York

Dimensions: 53'1" x 11'1" x 3'5"   **Tonnage:**   20

Date of Loss: Thursday, October 6, 1831

Cause of Loss: collision

Typical Sloop
Merchant Vessels of the Great Lakes

Story of the Loss:

While attempting to enter Fairport Harbor, Ohio during high seas, the *Olive Branch* struck the piers. An attempt at rescuing one of the crew failed when the fellow attempting the rescue had to be saved by yet a third man.

From the Painesville *Telegraph*, October 11, 1831:

> Much damage is reported to have been sustained on the lake during the week past. We have not many particulars on which reliance can be placed. The schr. *Olive Branch* was wrecked at the mouth of Grand River on Thursday morning last, by running against the pier while endeavoring to make the harbor. She was freighted principally with merchandise, which was nearly all lost. The crew got safely ashore.

As with many vessels lost in Lake Erie, rumors began to spring up that the *Olive Branch* was a treasure ship. Her cargo of general merchandise did include a limited amount of spirits. However, the stories of copper and gold are somewhat exaggerated. An article in *Lost Treasure* magazine published in February 1977 epitomizes these treasure tales. Not only does the article make up the cargo, it also gets all the dates wrong.

The Wreck Today:

What remains of the *Olive Branch* is buried in sand. Old time divers reportedly found a stove made in Geauga County, Ohio, as well as shoes on the wreckage. A few timbers are sometimes visible above the shifting sand. There is very heavy boat traffic in this area.

A public beach begins just east of the mouth of the Grand River, off where the wreck is located.

OLIVE BRANCH TREASURE

By Michael Hudson

In October of 1820, the Great Lakes shipping season was drawing to a close. The sloop **Olive Branch** had only to get into Fairport Harbor and unload her cargo before returning to her home port of Chicago.

This had been a long trip. In Duluth, several tons of copper ingots had been taken on board. At Sault Ste. Marie, one hundred cases of good Canadian whiskey, and finally, $2,000 in easily insurable gold specie destined for the Cleveland Trust Bank were also loaded.

Exactly why the ship piled into the marked reef at the mouth of the harbor is not known. That particular reef has claimed nearly 30 ships through the years, and many of these have been successfully salvaged.

However, Ohio in 1820 was little more than a wilderness, and by the time sophisticated diving techniques were developed, the **Olive Branch** was long forgotten. In fact, during three years of intensive research dealing mainly with wrecks off the Ohio shore of Lake Erie, I came across only one mention of the ship's loss.

An article in the October, 1820 Painesville *Sun* on microfilm at a local library, told of the disaster, listed the cargo, and also mentioned that the crew managed to swim ashore without the loss of a single life.

The **Olive Branch** no doubt lies under several feet of mud by now, but a salvage attempt could prove worthwhile—**Michael Hudson**

False treasure tale from Lost Treasure Magazine, February 1977.

CHARLES B. PACKARD

Official #: 135940   **Site #:** 82

Location: 7 miles west of Pelee passage

Coordinates: LORAN: 43808.6 57053.8   DGPS: 41 55.221 82 43.658

Lies: east-west   **Depth:** 40 feet

Type: propeller   **Cargo:** lumber

Power: steeple compound engine, scotch boiler

Owner(s) Leatham & Smith Towing and Wrecking Company

Built: 1887 at West Bay City, Michigan by F.W. Wheeler Company

Dimensions: 180'5" x 35'7" x 13'3"   **Tonnage:** 676 gross 504 net

Date of Loss: Sunday, September 16, 1906

Cause of Loss: struck the sunken vessel *Armenia*

Charles B. Packard

Historical Collections of the Great Lakes

Story of the Loss:

Originally named *Elfin-Mere*, her name was changed in 1902. A lamp exploded causing a fire at Green Bay, Wisconsin. The vessel was rebuilt as a crane equipped bulk freighter. The *Packard* spent her entire career as a workhorse hauling less glamorous cargoes (i.e. pulp wood) from smaller ports in the Great Lakes.

The year 1906 was not a very good year for Captain McCaffery. He almost lost the steamer *Joseph L. Hurd* when the vessel became waterlogged and nearly sank off Chicago. He then took command of the steamer *Charles B. Packard* and, four months after the schooner *Armenia* sank, the *Packard* struck her remains. Mortally wounded, the *Packard* tried to make it to shore but sank 45 minutes later in Pigeon Bay. There was no loss of life.

The Wreck Today:

Machinery and the propeller were salvaged before the remains of the *Packard* were dynamited to remove the navigation hazard. Today, the wreck is essentially a debris field with a large boiler. What remains of her hull sits upright in 40 feet of water. The silty bottom results in frequent poor visibility.

DOMINION OF CANADA.

NOTICE TO MARINERS.

No. 113 of 1906.

(INLAND NOTICE No. 26.)

All bearings, unless otherwise noted, are magnetic and are given from seaward, miles are nautical miles, heights are above high water, and all depths are at mean low water.

ONTARIO.

(271) Lake Erie—West end—Wreck off Kingsville.

The United States wooden propeller *Charles B. Packard* has sunk off Kingsville, in the west end of Lake Erie, in 6½ fathoms water, in a position fixed by the following sextant angles:

Pelee passage lighthouse	0°	7	miles distant.
Pelee island lighthouse	24	6½	" "
Hen island	51 50' 9⅞	" "

Lat.   N.   41° 55' 50"
Long. W.   82   41   30

N. to M. No. 113 (271) 10 10.06.

Source of information : Report from Capt. E. Dunn, C. G. S. Vigilant, 19th Sept., 1906.

This Canadian notice to mariners helped to locate and identify the Packard.

PENELOPE

Official #:	150582	**Site #:**	43
Location:	¼ mile off Avon Lake, Ohio		
Coordinates:	LORAN: 43730.5 57309.1	DGPS: 41 30.562 82 02.443	
Lies:	bow south	**Depth:**	8 feet
Type:	tug	**Cargo:**	light
Power:	propeller, steam fore and aft 2 cylinder		
Owner(s)	A.H. Langell of Cleveland, Ohio		
Built:	1892 at St. Clair, Michigan by Simon Langell		
Dimensions:	74' x 13'7" x 8'9"	**Tonnage:**	54.12 gross 35.5 net
Date of Loss:	Sunday, December 19, 1909		
Cause of Loss:	fire		

Penelope shortly after she sank
Gerry Duff Paine

Story of the Loss:

The *Penelope* was built as a pleasure craft with tapestries, silk, and leather cushions. She was sold to a possible relative of the builder and converted to a fish tug shortly before her loss.

While en route to winter lay up in St. Clair, Michigan, the *Penelope* encountered heavy weather and ice. Captain Inches decided to put into Lorain, Ohio. As he made the turn for Lorain, he noticed smoke coming from a forward hatch. Rushing forward, he found a blazing inferno. The engineer and fireman attempted to fight the fire with the hoses and Captain Inches headed the tug for shore at full speed. As the flames licked at the pilothouse, the three men attempted to launch their large lifeboat but watched it burn before their eyes. With the pilothouse engulfed in flames, the engineer Percival Upper dove down into the super heated engine room to slow the tug. Captain Inches, his hands burned and hair singed, ordered the small, partially burned yawl lowered.

Residents on shore had alerted the fire chief, who sent Great Lakes Towing Company tug *E.M. Pierce* to the rescue. Unable to reach the men in the yawl boat due to ice and shallow water, the *Pierce* attempted to tow the abandoned *Penelope* to deeper water. Failing this, she threw water on it as it drifted east into shallow water. As the survivors pulled for the beach, a cheering crowd on shore helped them land their yawl boat.

The Wreck Today:

On the shallow rock bottom, divers will find the *Penelope's* shaft, prop, cast ballast stones, tools, engine parts, metal rudder, and many nails and spikes. The 5 ½' x 10' boiler lies 100 feet north of the primary debris field. It is in 12 feet of water and comes within four feet of the surface. There is heavy boat and personal watercraft traffic in this area.

Left - Metal parts & balast stone in Penelope debris field Right- Penelope boiler - Photos by Georgann Wachter

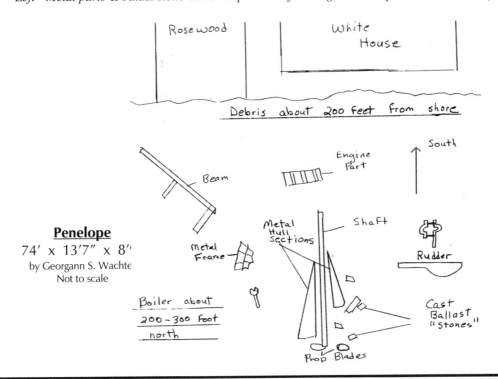

Zadock Pratt

Official #:   **Site #:**   64

Location: 3 miles south of Point Pelee
Coordinates: sorry, still secret
Lies: bow east and scattered   **Depth:**   25 feet
Type: schooner, 3 mast   **Cargo:**   wheat
Power: sail
Owner(s)   Morse and Captain Parker of Buffalo, New York
Built: 1855 at Buffalo, New York by Smith and Spencer
Dimensions: 133' x 26'10" x 10'11"   **Tonnage:**   370
Date of Loss: Tuesday, November 20, 1860
Cause of Loss: struck the sunken propeller *Mount Vernon*

Story of the Loss:

The *Zadock Pratt* possessed a talent for striking submerged objects. She ran aground 10 miles north of Milwaukee, Wisconsin in October 1856 and again at the Saint Clair flats in April 1859.

On Tuesday, November 20, 1860, the *Pratt* was downbound from Chicago when she ran foul of the sunken propeller *Mount Vernon*. The crew took to a small boat and was picked up by the schooner *J. S. Holly*. They were given refreshments and then landed on the Canadian shore.

The Wreck Today

The *Zadock Pratt* lies scattered in 25 feet of water. Her keelson and lower hull members are flat on the bottom and some small machinery and a pump from the wreck of the lie to the south of this structure. This debris is probably off the *Mount Vernon*, the remains of which lie immediately to the west of the *Zadock Pratt*. The bottom is sandy and there are many small fish and fresh water sponges.

CAUTION: There is often a strong current at this site.

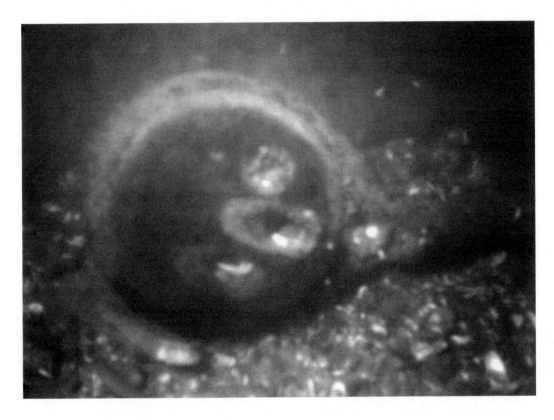

A deadeye peers through the misty water surrounding the Zadock Pratt. Photo by Georgann Wachter

John Pridgeon, Jr.

Official #:	75756	**Site #:**	39

Location: 5 miles NE of Avon Point, Avon Lake, Ohio
Coordinates: LORAN: 43775.7   57362.3   DGPS: 41.35.320   81.58.601
Lies: bow west   **Depth:** 60 feet
Type: wood propeller   **Cargo:** 1,000,000 feet of lumber
Power: 375 HP low pressure condensing 46x40 from Detroit Locomotive Works
Owner(s) Boland & Cornelius, Buffalo, New York
Built: 1875 at Detroit, Michigan by John P. Clark Company
Dimensions: 221'5" x 36'3" x 14'   **Tonnage:** 1173 gross   836 net
Date of Loss: Saturday, September 18, 1909
Cause of Loss: sprung leak in heavy seas

John Pridgeon, Jr and consorts
Great Lakes Historical Society

Story of the Loss:

Her engine was from the propeller *B. F. Wade*. Originally 1211.88 gross and 1037.71 net, she was rebuilt as bulk carrier at Buffalo, New York in 1902. In 1886 the *Pridgeon* was traveling in a fog and heavy gale off Sheboygan, Michigan when she struck and sunk the steam barge *Selah Chamberlain*.

Bound from Cutler, Ontario to Tonawanda, New York the *Pridgeon* had an uneventful voyage until encountering heavy seas about 12:00 noon. At that point Captain Hugh O'Hagan began testing with the pumps every five or six minutes. About 4:00, the first evidence of a leak was discovered. As O'Hagan tells it, "I made as close an examination of the hold as I could, but could not learn just where the leak started. The water gathered in the hold slowly at first, and we had no doubt but what we would be able to keep it under control with the pumps. I had no thought of danger when I went aft and ordered the men and women asleep in the after cabins to turn out for duty. It was a fortunate thing. They had hardly stepped out on deck when the leak suddenly increased and the boat listed violently to starboard. As it listed, the stern dropped out and the cabins in which the people had been sleeping went overboard with a rush."

As the rising water extinguished her boiler fire, the last bit of steam was used to sound distress calls. Responding to these signals, the steamer *Maryland* rescued the crew of twelve men and two women without incident. As the rescued crew was taken to Cleveland, the *Pridgeon's* consort schooner *Case* anchored near the sunken vessel overnight.

The Wreck Today:

The vessel lies twisted in 60 feet of water. While her stern is almost turtled, much of the vessel is on its port side. Her large propeller and her engine are interesting to explore. To the south of the main structure, about midwreck, there is a large north/south timber section land a tree. A trademark of this site are the many huge timbers, undoubtedly from her cargo.

In recent years, the bow section has completely collapsed, leaving her bow stem carving a lonely figure out of the silt. The wreck continues to rapidly deteriorate. Care must be taken when diving this wreck! Frequent low visibility makes it possible to accidentally penetrate this aging shipwreck..

Clockwise from top left: pony boiler and steel arch, propeller, bow stem. Video captures by Mike Wachter

F.H . PRINCE

Official #:   120797   **Site #:**   88

Location: ½ mile off the east side of Kelleys Island

Coordinates: LORAN: 43683.0   57000.4   DGPS: 41 36.240   82 40.520

Lies: bow west   **Depth:**   18 feet

Type: propeller   **Cargo:**   sand

Power: fore and aft compound engine

Owner(s)   Lake Erie Sand and Gravel

Built: 1890 at Detroit, Michigan by Detroit Dry Dock

Dimensions: 240' x 42' x 23'4"   **Tonnage:**   2047 gross 1547 net

Date of Loss: Tuesday, August 8, 1911

Cause of Loss: fire

F. H. Prince
Great Lakes Historical Society

Story of the Loss:

Built as a package freighter, the *Prince* was converted to a sand dredge in 1910.

As the steamer *F.H. Prince* passed six miles off the United States Coast Guard Station at Marblehead, Ohio on the morning of Tuesday, August 8, those on watch observed fire on her bow. Unable to successfully quell the flames, Captain H.H. Parsons drove the *Prince* on to the beach on the east shore of Kelleys island shortly after she caught fire. In an attempt to save the ship, sandsuckers *Mary H* and *Albert Y. Gowan* pumped water on her but her heavily damaged bow prevented the vessel from being pulled free. Lifesavers from the coast guard station were dispatched to remove the crew of the *Prince* from the grounded vessel.

Following the fire, Captain Parsons stated his belief that the vessel was not beyond repair. However, the Homegardner Sand Company seeking payment for fighting the fire placed a salvage claim on the *Prince*. As a result, federal officials seized the vessel before she could be removed. On the following Sunday night, brisk winds fanned the still smoldering timbers of the *Prince* and fire again swept across the ill-fated sandsucker and destroyed what remained of the vessel.

The Wreck Today:

The engine and boilers were removed in 1914. However, many heavy timbers remain and there is machinery that comes within 2 feet of the surface. The wreckage lies on a rock bottom and is home to many fish. As a result, many fishermen frequent her and the wreckage is smothered with monofilament and lures. If you can fend off the heavy boat traffic, this is a great place to pick up fishing tackle.

Schools of fish frequent the F.H. Prince.

Machinery comes within two feet of the surface..

Fresh water sponges cover the charred timbers.

Small sections of decking remain.

Video captures by Mike Wachter

QUEEN OF THE WEST

Official #:	20584	**Site #:**	5
Location:	8 miles north of Fairport, Ohio		
Coordinates:	LORAN: 43986.1 57735.0	DGPS: 41 50.768 82 23.135	
Lies:	bow west	**Depth:**	876 gross 588 net
Type:	wood propeller	**Cargo:**	iron ore
Power:	steam engine		
Owner(s)	C.L. Hutchinson, Cleveland, Ohio		
Built:	1881 at Bay City, Michigan by William Crosthwaite		
Dimensions:	215' x 32'6" x 16'4"	**Tonnage:**	876 gross 588 net
Date of Loss:	Thursday, August 20, 1903		
Cause of Loss:	foundered in storm		

Queen of the West
Historical Collections of the Great Lakes

Story of the Loss:

Launched March 16, 1881, her original tonnage was 818.84 gross, 625 net. Her tonnage changed after a 1901 rebuild in Cleveland, Ohio.

Bound from Escanaba, Michigan to Erie, Pennsylvania, the *Queen of the West* had dropped her consorts *H.W. Sage* and *May Richards* in Cleveland at 12:20 a.m.   Continuing on to Erie as the wind was "breezing up from the northeast" she encountered building seas. By 3:00 a.m., the seas were breaking over the vessel and shortly after 4:00, the crew discovered she was taking on water. Captain S.B. Massey ordered the pumps put into action. According to a member of the crew, "By that time we were nearly down to Fairport and about five miles off the land. She rolled so heavily and the seas broke over her to such an extent that we had to bring her head into it and check down. We attempted to launch our lifeboat but lost it. The sea was breaking up everything on deck."

Responding to the stricken boat's distress signal, the steamer *Codorus* rushed to the sinking vessel to take the crew off. The *Queen of the West* turned to approach the *Codorus* and Misses Jennie & Mabel Drouilland, daughters of the engineer, were almost washed overboard by heavy seas that swept the boat. Fortunately, they were rescued without injury. As wheelsman Patrick Maloney jumped from the *Queen*, he fell between the two vessels. Although he survived, his breast and three ribs were crushed. No other injuries were reported.

The Wreck Today:

Captain Motley of the Cleveland Lifesaving crew found the pilothouse of the *Queen of the West* almost 30 miles away from the wreck site, near the Cleveland crib. The *Queen* lies upright in 70 feet of water. As she was salvaged with a clamshell, little decking is intact. Despite this, she is truly a majestic sight. Her engines, boiler, windlass, and winches sit as though ready to sail again. There is some fishnet around the stern and portions of the stern have collapsed.

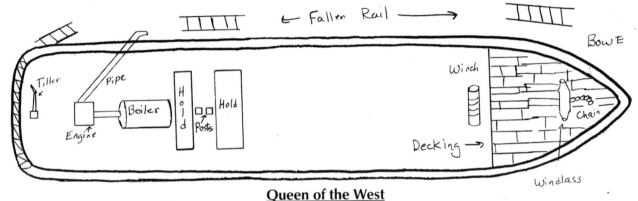

Queen of the West
215' x 32'6" x 16'4"
by Georgann S. Wachter
not to scale

Windlass wheel at the bow. Video capture by Mike Wachter

QUITO

Official #:   6768   **Site #:**   48

Location: just east of the breakwaters at Lorain, Ohio

Coordinates: LORAN: 43696.5   57232.3

Lies: scattered   **Depth:**   10 - 22 feet

Type: wood propeller   **Cargo:**   iron ore

Power: steam engine

Owner(s)   James Corrigan of Cleveland, Ohio

Built: 1873 by Thomas Boston, Bangor, Michigan

Dimensions: 204' x 36'2" x 21'7"   **Tonnage:**   1372 gt 1099 net

Date of Loss: Tuesday, November 25, 1902

Cause of Loss: grounded

Quito
Historical Collections of the Great Lakes

Story of the Loss:

Launched April 16, 1873 as the *David Ballentine* under command of Captain Mansfield, she sank in Lake Superior in 1890. The vessel was raised and renamed *Quito* by chewing gum magnate, W.J. White. She was shortened and her tonnage changed (1394 gross, 1206 net) at the James Davidson Shipyard in West Bay City, Michigan, June 24, 1890. Her tonnage was again changed (1372 gross, 1099 net) September 1, 1890 at Cleveland, Ohio.

Used mostly in the iron ore trade, the *Quito* is named for Quito, Equador, the oldest capital city in South America. Original dimensions 221' x 37'1" x 13'5", 972 gross 595 net.

Battling a northeast gale, the *Quito* was carrying iron ore from Escanaba, Michigan to Cleveland, Ohio and had passed Lorain when Captain Hugh S. Cody discovered water in the hold. As his pumps made no headway on the 4 feet of water in the hold, Cody turned back to Lorain. Unable to enter the harbor in the gale, Cody cruised past the harbor mouth blowing his whistle as a signal for assistance. As the tugs *Cascade* and *Steadman* responded the crew lost control of the vessel. The *Quito* grounded hard on the bow as her stern continued to swing with the wind and waves. The captain and most of the crew leapt to safety on the *Cascade*. However, four crewmen who had gone below to collect their belongings were inadvertently left on board the dying vessel. Returning to the *Quito*, the tugs were able to rescue one more crewman before the gale forced their return to harbor.

A call for help went to the Cleveland lifesaving crew. The B&O Railroad provided a train of two cars and a caboose to carry the Cleveland crew and their equipment (boat, cannon, and ropes) to Lorain. Captain Motley and crew arrived at 11:00 pm. Shortly before midnight the small lifesaving boat was launched against the surging waves inside the breakwater. Spectators rushed to the water's edge to watch as the tiny vessel was tossed by monster waves outside the breakwalls. Indistinguishable from the white foam of the waves, all that could be seen of the white surfboat was the lantern as they crested each wave. Then, as the lifeboat rounded the stricken *Quito*, it was lost from view entirely. Many believed the seas had driven it under. Finally, the lifeboat returned. Not only was the lifesaving crew uninjured, they also had aboard the remaining three crewmen of the *Quito*. But for the heroic efforts of Captain Motley and his lifesaving crew, these three would most certainly have perished in the storm.

The Wreck Today:

The machinery and iron ore from the *Quito* were salvaged and what little remained of the vessel was leveled. Today, no large pieces of the wreck remain. Metal and wood parts are scattered over a large area in 12 to 22 feet of water. In 1966 the ships clock was dredged up by the *William Denny* and donated to the Dossin Museum in Detroit. Several years later, a novice scuba diver found her compass. It was in perfect working order and looked like it had never been underwater. The remains of at least one other wreck are scattered in the same location. Watch for heavy boat and personal watercraft traffic.

RAPHAEL

Official #: 266980   **Site #:** 4

Location: 333°T 23 miles off Fairport, Ohio

Coordinates: GPS: position approximate: 42°04'50"   81°25'50"

Lies: east/weat   **Depth:** 80 feet

Type: barge   **Cargo:** steel bars, billets, & ingots of pig iron

Power: towed

Owner(s) Reliance Marine Transportation and Construction

Built: 1954 at Kingston, New York by Reliance Marine Transportation & Construction

Dimensions: 107.7' x 42.5' x 13.8'   **Tonnage:** 643

Date of Loss: Tuesday, July 12, 1966

Cause of Loss: cargo shifted in storm

Tecumsah II, barge similar to the Raphael
Author's Collection

Story of the Loss:

The Great Lakes Towing Company's 97 foot tug *Superior* had dropped the barge *Rita* in Buffalo, New York at the Republic Steel Company dock. She took the barge *Raphael* in tow for the return trip to Detroit, Michigan. The barge was covered with tarpaulins and secured for the cross lake trip.

Radio static prevented the *Superior* from receiving weather reports. As the tow proceeded the seas increased and the *Superior* checked down her speed on two occasions. Now traveling at only 3 miles per hour she and her tow were encountering winds of 30 miles per hour from the west. These winds built waves ranging from 5 to 8 feet high.

Shortly before 10:00 p.m. a scowman reported the *Raphael* was listing. Captain Walter Karhu immediately ordered the crew to stand by with axes to cut the 400 foot towline. At 10:15 p.m. the barge's cargo shifted even further causing her to heal hard to port and sink. Fortunately the captain, his 7 man crew and the two scowmen were all aboard the *Superior*. Released from the sunken tow, the tug took refuge in Ashtabula, Ohio. Attempts to locate the barge using aircraft equipped with a magnetometer were unsuccessful. However, the search did discover the *James B. Colgate*, a victim of the Black Friday Storm of 1916.

The Wreck Today

The *Raphael* had one hatch, a pushing notch at the stern, and a small crew's quarters below deck on the port side.   The vessel appears to be completely intact. However, she is on her side and buried deep in the mud. There is no easy way to access her and it would take significant excavation to explore anything other than her exterior sides.

RELIEF

Official #:	21133	**Site #:**	90
Location:	Carpenters Point, west tip of Kelleys Island		
Coordinates:	GPS position approximate 41.36. 00, 82.44.33		
Lies:	scattered	**Depth:**	12 feet
Type:	tug	**Cargo:**	none
Power:	steam engine		
Owner(s)	J.C. Gilchrist, Gilchrist Transportation Company		
Built:	1855 at Buffalo, New York by VanSlyke and Notter		
Dimensions:	127'2" x 25'5" x 12'11"	**Tonnage:**	267 gross 134 net
Date of Loss:	Friday, July 18, 1884		
Cause of Loss:	fire		

Relief
Private collection of Ralph Roberts

Story of the Loss:

The large tug *Relief* was responsible for salvaging the *Morning Star* after the terrible collision between the steamer and the bark *Cortland*. In June of 1868, working in 60 feet of water, divers from the *Relief* salvaged pig iron, glass, cheese, and personal items belonging to the passengers and crew of the *Morning Star*. By attaching large wood casks to the hull of the sunken steamer and then filling the casks with air, the *Relief* was able to raise the *Morning Star*. She was towed approximately 9 miles when, without forewarning, she sank again, taking two carpenters with her. In the photo of the *Relief* taken in Buffalo, New York, you can see a diver going over the side of the ship.

Late in the evening of Friday, July 18, 1884, the *Relief* caught fire near Starve Island Reef. The first alarm was issued by engineer James Baker after an explosion of gas forward of the engine room. The flames shot through the aging tug so rapidly that Captain C.E. Chiltson and his 11 member crew were forced to jump overboard. One fireman was badly burned before escaping the blazing vessel. All members of the crew were rescued by a rowboat launched from a nearby island and by the tug *Cal Davis*.

The burned hull was towed to the west end of Kelleys Island. There it settled to the bottom.

The Wreck Today:

The *Cal Davis* claimed salvage rights and removed some of the machinery. In August of 1913 the boiler was removed. More recently, divers have reported shallow remains of timbers on the rocky bottom at Carpenters Point.

The tug Relief works to salvage the Morning Star. Watercolor by Georgann Wachter.

ROBERT

Official #: 254623   **Site #:** 16

Location: 5 miles south of Erieau, Ontario

Coordinates: LORAN: 44044.2 57510.5   DGPS: 42 13.094 81 58.937

Lies: bow east   **Depth:** 49 feet

Type: steel fish tug   **Cargo:** fish

Power: 130 horsepower deisel engine

Owner(s) Captain Sam Aikens of Blenheim, Ontario

Built: 1948 at Vermilion, Ohio

Dimensions: 38'3" x 13.1' x 4.8'   **Tonnage:** 12 gross 9 net

Date of Loss: Sunday, September 26, 1982

Cause of Loss: collision

Robert

Lakelore

Story of the Loss:

The four man crew of the fish tug were in the process of setting nets when another fish tug, the *B. M. Cabral* of Wheatley, collided with the vessel. The *Robert* sunk in less than two minutes. Captain Sam Aikens and crew jumped off the doomed vessel and were picked up by Captain David Cabral and the crew of the other tug. Captain Aikens reported, "In my 35 years on the lake I have never heard of such a thing happening ... We are just lucky to be alive."

The Wreck Today:

Located on a rock bottom, the *Robert* was surrounded by two pleasure craft that were intentionally sunk next to her in 1995. Unfortunately, these vessels, the *Largo Pariso* and *Racers Edge*, are reported to have collapsed.

On the *Robert*, there is some net, radar, autopilot, and fish boxes.

SAINT LAWRENCE

Official #: 22348   **Site #:** 48

Location: ¾ mile east of Lorain Harbor, Ohio

Coordinates: LORAN: 43697.2 57234.2   DGPS:

Lies: scattered   **Depth:** 20 feet

Type: schooner   **Cargo:** coal

Power: sail

Owner(s) Captain John D. Baker of Detroit

Built: 1863 at Cleveland, Ohio by Quayle & Martin

Dimensions: 137.1' x 26' x 11.5'   **Tonnage:** 281.16 gross 267.11 net

Date of Loss: Wednesday, November 21, 1900

Cause of Loss: storm

Saint Lawrence

Great Lakes Historical Society

Story of the Loss:

Originally bark rigged, the *Saint Lawrence* was rebuilt in 1876 at Port Huron, Michigan.

During a ferocious snowstorm, the *Saint Lawrence* tried to take shelter at Lorain Harbor. The tug *Christ Grover* came out and attempted to throw her a line but was forced to retreat by the weather. Captain Baker deployed his anchors. Unfortunately, they would not hold and the ship continued to drift toward shore until it grounded. A yawl boat was launched and the Captain, his wife, two sons and a daughter went ashore. Onlookers helping the yawl come ashore learned that four men were still aboard.

The lifesaving station at Cleveland Harbor had been alerted and brought a surfboat and life car by special train. Reaching the scene late in the afternoon, the lifesaving crew attempted a breeches buoy rescue. However, the four men clinging to the mainmast did not have the strength to haul out the whip. As this was unsuccessful, the surfboat was put out and rescued the freezing sailors. Later that night, the *Saint Lawrence* broke in two.

A former owner of the *Saint Lawrence*, Captain George Chilsen, watched from his lakefront home as the waves splintered the once proud vessel. The photo on the previous page shows the endangered ship at anchor shortly before she sank.

The Wreck Today:

The wreck lies widely scattered on a sand and rock bottom. There is a large stock anchor, wood, and many metal parts. The steamer *Quito* sunk in this same area in 1902 and pieces of the two wrecks are intermingled on the bottom.

Watch for heavy boat traffic.

SAINT LOUIS

Official #:	none	**Site #:**	85
Location:	1½ miles NE of Kelleys Island		
Coordinates:	LORAN: 43705.2 57030.7		
Lies:	Scattered	**Depth:**	20 feet
Type:	sidewheel steamer	**Cargo:**	passengers, miscellaneous
Power:	cross-head engine, 28' diameter wheels		freight and livestock
Owner(s)	John Hollister and others		
Built:	1844 at Perrysburgh, Ohio by Samuel Hubbell		
Dimensions:	190'1" x 27'5" x 12'4"	**Tonnage:**	618
Date of Loss:	Sunday, November 7, 1852		
Cause of Loss:	grounded in storm		

Saint Louis
Drawing by Georgann Wachter

Story of the Loss:

The engine of the *Saint Louis* came from Sandusky and was installed in Cleveland.

On her run from Buffalo, New York to Detroit, Michigan, the *Saint Louis* was blown on the rocks near Kelleys Island. The passengers reached the island and were taken off by the *Northern Indiana* the following day.

The same storm sank the steamers *Princeton* and *Oneida* at the east end of Lake Erie.

The Wreck Today:

The engine was removed and the hull burned. Some scattered remains, including a boiler, can be found along the rock bottom. This area has very heavy boat traffic and the shallow shoals present an additional hazard.

Sand Merchant

Official #:	C153443	**Site #:**	38

Location: 4 miles NE of Avon Point, Avon Lake, Ohio

Coordinates: LORAN: 43771.7   57368.3   DGPS: 41 34.428   81 57.524

Lies:	Bow southeast	**Depth:**	65 feet
Type:	Steel sandsucker	**Cargo:**	sand

Power: Triple Expansion Engine; 15½" 26"x44" diameter x 26" stroke

Owner(s) National Sand and Material Company, Ltd., Toronto, Canada   Hull #: 79

Built: 1927 at Collingwood, Ontario, Canada by Collingwood Shipbuilding Company

Dimensions:	252' x 43'6" x 17'5"	**Tonnage:**	1981 gross

Date of Loss: Saturday, October 17, 1936

Cause of Loss: foundered

Sand Merchant
Great Lakes Historical Society

Story of the Loss:

Interlake Transportation Company, Ltd. contracted for the *Sand Merchant* March 12, 1927. Her keel was laid April 28 and she was launched August 17, 1927. Her maiden voyage from Collingwood, Ontario began September 12, 1927.

The *Sand Merchant* was constructed with two open hopper sided holds. Sand and gravel were pumped on board by two centrifugal pumps. Mounted aft of the forecastle and forward of the stack were two derricks with two yard grab buckets. These were used for offloading until they were replaced in 1930 by an elevator system and a conveyor belt discharge.

Sand Merchant

In 1931, Royal Trust Company, Montreal, acquired the *Merchant* from Mapes and Fredon to operate under charter to National Sand and Materials Company, Ltd. She saw limited duty in 1932 and none at all in 1933. Returned to service in 1934, she operated on the lakes and on the Canadian east coast until her loss.

On October 17, 1936, while en route for Cleveland from Point Pelee with a load of sand, the *Sand Merchant* developed a list at about 8:30 p.m. By 9:30, the wind was picking up, the lake was choppy, and the list was increasing. Shortly before 10:00, Captain Graham MacClelland ordered the lifeboats lowered. As the boats were lowered, 17 miles northwest of Cleveland, the *Sand Merchant* overturned. According to Captain MacClelland, "The *Sand Merchant* is an open hatched ship. Waves were weighing down the sand, so I ordered everyone into the boats. I stood on the bridge and gave the signal for the boats to be lowered. At the same time, I jumped without a life preserver, just before the ship capsized."

As she sank, both of her lifeboats were overturned in what was now a 50 mile per hour gale with 15 foot waves. In his leap to the water, the captain was knocked unconscious. A sailor dragged him by the hair to an overturned lifeboat. Clinging desperately to the lifeboats in the numbing waters, the majority of the crew lost their grips on the lifeboats, and their lives. Eighteen men and one woman perished. For ten dark, storm ridden hours, they watched unseeing ships pass them by. Finally, as dawn broke, the capsized and drifting lifeboats were spotted five miles off of Cleveland by the steamer *Thunder Bay Quarries*.

Four survivors were hauled aboard the *Marquette & Bessimer No. 1* and taken to Cleveland. The steamer *Thunder Bay Quarries* took the captain and two other survivors to Sandusky, Ohio.

Captain MacClelland, Herman Dault, and John Udeson after rescue from overturned lifeboat.
Lorain Journal and Times Herald, Monday October 19, 1936

In November 1936, a Toronto wreck commissioner exonerated Captain MacClelland of any blame. However, he was censured for failing to have lifeboat drills and permitting an unauthorized person on board.

The Wreck Today:

The *Sand Merchant* lies upside down in the mud with her dominant features, the prop and rudder, to the northwest. There is a deep trench around the wreck and a truly reckless diver could get into the wreck by going around the rails at the bottom of the trench. We would not recommend this, as it is likely the mud around the entry would collapse and doubtful that the diver would be able to find a way back out. One of her cranes lies along her starboard side. To the west of the wreck is a large debris field. This contains many ships parts, including a deck crane, the spotlight, and whistle. Large sand piles lay among the debris.

The vessel was never salvaged. In 1995 a group of adventurers from Avon Lake, Ohio filed for a permit to cut her hull open in order to gain entry to the vessel. We do not know if the permit was issued.

The loading crain and air scoop lie among scattered wreckage in the Sand Merchant's debris field.

Author Georgann Wachter explores the loading crain.

Video captures by Mike Wachter

SARAH E. SHELDON

Official #: 115053   **Site #:** 47

Location: ½ mile off Sheffield Lake, Ohio

Coordinates: LORAN: 43713.8 57268.6   DGPS: 41 29.741   82 06.678

Lies: bow east   **Depth:** 20 feet

Type: propeller   **Cargo:** coal

Power: steeple compound engine

Owner(s) M.A. Bradley, Cleveland, Ohio

Built: 1872 at Lorain, Ohio by Quelos & Peck

Dimensions: 184' 1" x 32'4" x 13'8"   **Tonnage:** 693.42 gross 517.23 net

Date of Loss: Friday, October 20, 1905

Cause of Loss: grounded in storm

Sarah E. Sheldon
Historical Collections of the Great Lakes

Story of the Loss:

Built for S. Sheldon, she was sold to Lucy A. Russell of Cleveland who purchased the schooner *Samuel P. Ely* as a consort for the *Sheldon*. In 1884, she was sold to M.A. Bradley of the Bradley Transportation Company. On September 16, 1886, the *Sheldon* caught fire and was badly burned while in the Cuyahoga River. Later in her career, she picked up the *Neguanee* as a consort and went from the grain trade to the lumber trade. She was rebuilt in March of 1894.

It was late Thursday evening, October 19, as the *Sarah E. Sheldon* took on a load of coal to be carried from Cleveland to Sarnia, Ontario. Being a superstitious man, Captain Garant hastened his sailing, thinking a Friday departure unlucky. The boat left Cleveland just before midnight. First stop, Huron, to pick up her consort, *Neguanee*.

After the *Sheldon* passed Avon Point, a full gale developed out of the southwest. Captain Garant brought the vessel close to the lee shore for protection. At 5:00 a.m., the engineer reported that the *Sheldon* was "leaking worse than usual." As the vessel altered course for Lorain, the water gained on her boilers. She grounded offshore and began to break up. Realizing all was lost, Garant ordered the ship abandoned and tied the whistle cord down. This alerted a resident on shore to the ship's plight.

Two crewmen were washed to sea as they attempted to launch the yawl on the windward side of the boat. Arriving from Lorain, the tug *Kunkle Brothers* found the surviving crew clinging to the masts. Captain Garant signaled the tug to search for the lost crewmen. The tug returned to the *Sheldon*, unsuccessful in the search. Five of *Sheldon's* crew jumped aboard the tug before the tug captain, feeling his vessel endangered by the shallow water, left the area.

Meanwhile, Captain Motley of the Cleveland lifesaving crew had set out behind the tug *Frank W*. Using the *Frank W* as an anchor, the lifeboat was played out on a line and the rest of the grounded vessels crew was saved. "I tell you, it looked for a time as if someone would have to come out and rescue the lifesavers. ... When a big wave would strike up, we would be fifteen feet above the steamer, looking down upon her decks." Three years after the rescue, the tug crew received the Carnegie Medal for saving the crew of the *Sheldon*.

One of the worst storms ever on the Great Lakes, this gale also claimed the schooner *Tasmania* off Pelee Point and the steamer *Siberia* at Long Point. Several other vessels had close calls that night.

The Wreck Today:

The *Sheldon* lies scattered on a rocky bottom in 20 feet of water. Her huge propeller angles off to the starboard side of the wreck. Unfortunately two of the blades have come off (some say by ice, others say the blades were cut by divers). The small capstan that used to lay 12 kicks south of the eastern end of the keel has been moved next to the propeller. A large capstan lies several hundred feet to the east of the keel section. The site has abundant metal and lots of bass. We call these "attack bass" as they are very protective of their eggs during spawning season. Slightly to the northeast is a large section of the vessel's side. To the southeast there is additional wreckage. Her boiler is on shore to the west of the wreck site.

CAUTION: This wreck lies directly in the path from the CEI power plant at Avon Lake and Lorain Harbor. As a result, there is often boat traffic in the area. A DIVE FLAG IS ABSOLUTELY REQUIRED!

*Like most shallow water shipwrecks, the
Sheldon is home to many fish.*
Photo by Georgann Wachter

GENERAL FRANZ SIGEL

Official #: 10217   **Site #:** 102

Location: 75°T 4.5 miles off the Monroe, Michigan Breakwater

Coordinates: PA: 41 54.50   81 14.95

Lies: **Depth:** 28 feet

Type: schooner   **Cargo:** coal

Power: three masted sail

Owner(s) Wilfred J. Curtis of Lorain, Ohio

Built: 1863 on the Black River, Ohio by Henry D. Root

Dimensions: 136.8' x 25.8' x 11.5'   **Tonnage:** 360 gross 301.06 net

Date of Loss: Saturday, July 18, 1903

Cause of Loss: sprung a leak in a storm

General Franz Sigel
Great Lakes Historical Society

Story of the Loss:

The *General Franz Sigel* was built during the Civil War. She bore the name of a German born general who hailed from Saint Louis, Missouri and commanded the 11th and 12th Army Corps. In November of 1882 the *Sigel* went ashore in Lake Michigan at Big Point Sable. Prematurely declared a total loss, she was raised and sailed for 11 more years..

On Friday, July 17, 1903, Captain Will Curtis was guiding the *Sigel* through a heavy northwest sea from Huron, Ohio to the coal dock at Sandwich Point when she sprang a leak. No one noticed her distress until the following morning, by which time the crew had taken to the rigging. The government survey vessel *Williams* steamed to the rescue of the exhausted crew. Captain Curtis saved only the canvas and abandoned the *Sigel*. On boarding the *Williams*, Curtis stated that he felt he had just stepped out of a watery grave. The *Williams* took Curtis, his wife (the cook), mate W.D. McGregor, and two sailors to Toledo, Ohio.

The Wreck Today

In July of 1904 the U.S. dredge *Maumee* dynamited the wreck and dredged up the coal cargo as well as part of the hull. As a result, very little structure remains at this site. However, her debris field still offers exciting finds.

General Franz Sigel after she sank
Gerry Duff Paine

CHARLES SPADEMAN

Official #: 125158   **Site #:** 92

Location: 2/3 mile 160° from South Bass Island Lighthouse

Coordinates: LORAN: 28853.3 56920.1

Lies: scattered   **Depth:** 32 feet

Type: schooner   **Cargo:** coal

Power: towed

Owner(s) M. Sickens of Marine City, Michigan

Built: 1873 at Marine City, Michigan by Philip Rice

Dimensions: 134'2" x 25'9" x 10'8"   **Tonnage:** 306 gross 291 net

Date of Loss: Friday, December 10, 1909

Cause of Loss: cut by ice

Charles Spademan
Historical Collections of the Great Lakes

Story of the Loss:

Upbound to Marine City, Michigan, the *Charles Spademan* was in tow of the steamer *Huron City* when they left Huron, Ohio on Friday afternoon, December 10, 1909. Severe ice was encountered as the two vessels approached the Lake Erie Islands. Believing the ice to be thin, the *Huron City* stayed her course until close to 6:00 p.m. Then, a decision was made to return to Huron. Sometime between 8:00 and 9:00 p.m. Captain James Bond of the *Spademan* noticed his ship had been cut by the ice and was leaking badly.

Within ten minutes, there was four feet of water in the hold. The crew kept at the pumps until the water had risen to eight feet. At that time, Captain Bond advised Captain Rivard aboard the *Huron City* of his vessels condition. The steamer put about, lashed the sinking schooner to her side and put down lines for the schooner's crew to climb. Captain Bond, Mate Frank Robinson, the cook Miss Struebling, and a seaman scrambled to safety. Ten minuets after they abandoned their ship, the *Spademan* settled to the bottom in 30 feet of water.

However, their safety was not yet secured. The *Huron City* had great difficulty getting back to Huron. Several miles of heavy ice lay between the vessel and safe harbor. Plowing into the ice, the wooden vessel was fortunate to be able to cut through without stoving her bow and suffering the same cruel fate as her consort.

Given the other events of the week, the crew of the *Spademan* can be considered to be lucky. She was the only one of four vessels lost during a particularly hostile week of December that had no casualties. The *Clarion, Marquette & Bessimer #2,* and the *W.C. Richardson* all were lost and were not so fortunate as to have no loss of life.

The Wreck Today:

The wreck was dynamited in April of 1910 and Captain E.J. Dodge removed her cargo of coal by clamshell. What little remains of the vessel is scattered across the rock bottom.

CAUTION: Watch for heavy boat traffic.

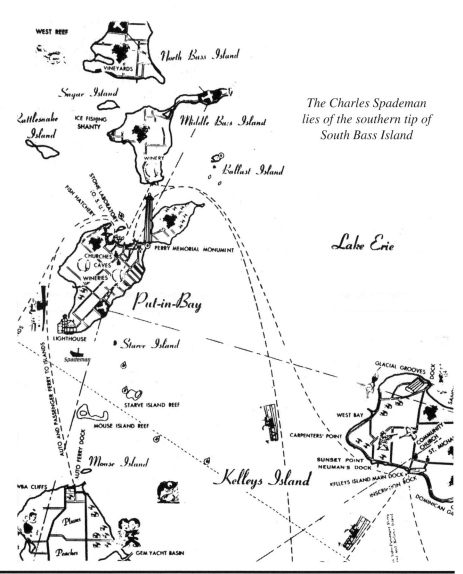

The Charles Spademan lies of the southern tip of South Bass Island

SPECULAR

Official #:   115876   **Site #:**   71

Location: 5 miles east of the northern tip of Pelee Island

Coordinates: LORAN: 43795.7   57128.3   DGPS: 41 49.335   82 32.165

Lies: bow west   **Depth:**   36 feet

Type: propeller   **Cargo:**   iron ore

Power: steam engine

Owner(s)   Republic Iron Company, Cleveland, Ohio

Built: 1882 at Cleveland, Ohio by George Presley and Company

Dimensions: 263'7" x 34'8" x 20'1"   **Tonnage:**   1741 gross 1439 net

Date of Loss: Wednesday, August 22, 1900

Cause of Loss: collision

Specular
Historical Collections of the Great Lakes

Story of the Loss:

Originally built as a schooner, the *Specular* was rebuilt as a steamer in 1888. She carried specular, a high grade iron ore, from the Michigan ranges to Cleveland.

Downbound from Marquette, Michigan, the *Specular* dropped her consort, the barge *Magnetic*, and proceeded to Cleveland. In the dark of a clear night, she collided with the propeller *Denver*. The *Denver* continued on her trip to Port Huron, somehow unaware that she had sunk another vessel. As the *Specular* took on water rapidly, most of her crew abandoned her. Other sailors had to take refuge in her rigging. They were all picked up by the steamer *Montana* and taken to Cleveland, Ohio.

The Wreck Today:

There is a large anchor and the engine lays exposed, as the sides have collapsed outward. Other notable features are the large boiler, firebox, and four bladed prop lying on the sand.

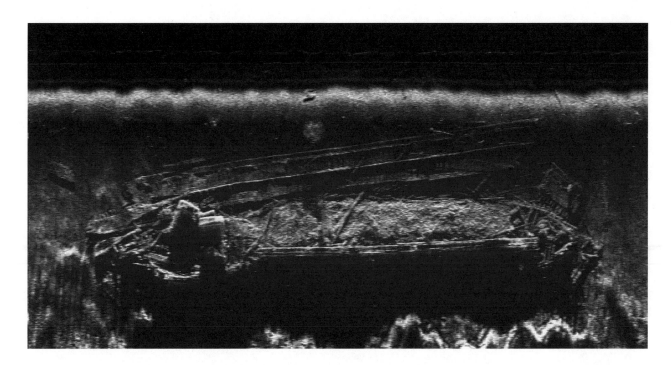

Sidescan image of the Specular wreck site.
Aqua Vision Research

Sternless

Official #:   **Site #:**   12

Location: 17 miles SE of Erieau, Ontario

Coordinates: LORAN: 44071.1   57673.8   DGPS: 42 08.375   81 37.942

Lies: bow west   **Depth:**   83 feet

Type: schooner, 3 masts   **Cargo:**

Power: sail

Owner(s)

Built:

Dimensions: approximately 128′ x 25′   **Tonnage:**

Date of Loss:

Cause of Loss: foundered

Stampede
similar to the Sternless

Story of the Loss:

Unknown, however, evidence indicates at least one crewman went down with the wreck. A capstan plate recovered from the wreck by survey teams indicates Talcott & Underhill of Oswego, New York made the capstan. Talcott and Underhill was founded 1853 and shortly thereafter became Ames Iron Works. As research into the identity of this wreck continues, the capstan plate helps narrow the date of the vessels construction to the mid to late 1850's.

The Wreck Today:

This unidentified schooner sits on a mud bottom. Fishnets have torn away part of her stern, hence the name "Sternless".

Look for her port anchor, windlass, capstan, and pumps.

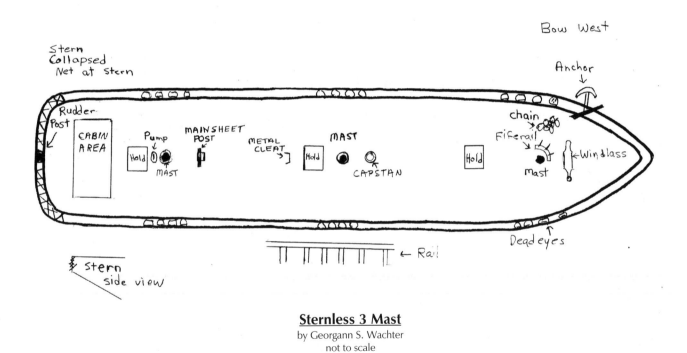

Sternless 3 Mast
by Georgann S. Wachter
not to scale

DAVID STEWART

Official #:	6144	**Site #:**	76
Location:	west side of Point Pelee		
Coordinates:	LORAN: 43858.0 57160.2	DGPS: 41 58.692 82 32.940	
Lies:	bow north	**Depth:**	25 feet
Type:	schooner	**Cargo:**	iron ore
Power:	sail		
Owner(s)	J.W. Squires of Marine City, Michigan		
Built:	1867 at Cleveland, Ohio by E.M. Peck		
Dimensions:	171' x 31' x 13'	**Tonnage:**	545
Date of Loss:	Friday, October 6, 1893		
Cause of Loss:	at anchor in a gale, blown aground		

David Stewart
Ralph Roberts' Collection

Story of the Loss:

The *David Stewart* was named for the president of the Jackson Iron Company of Marquette and Superior. In October 1891, she went aground 13 miles east of Fairport Harbor, Ohio, but was able to work herself free.

Bound from Escanaba, Michigan to Cleveland, Ohio, the *Stewart* encountered a heavy gale and sought shelter in Pigeon Bay. She anchored to ride out the storm and was riding safely until early afternoon. The wind shifted out of the southwest and increased in velocity causing the vessel to drag anchor and come aground 250 yards from shore about two miles below Leamington, Ontario. As darkness descended, the yawl boat was lost. About 11:00 p.m. Captain Titus sprang to the foremast and his crew were forced to cling to the mizzen mast for safety. At daylight, shore observers saw the mizzen mast swaying. No lifeboats were to be found. However, local fishermen were able to get word of the situation to the tug *Louise,* which lay at anchor opposite the *Stewart* on the east side of Point Pelee. Immediately on hearing the news, the captain of the *Louise,* got underway and, with great difficulty, saved the seven crewmen of the *Stewart* taking them to the safety of Sandusky Harbor. This earned the *Louise* high praise from the surviving crewmembers.

The *Louise* continued to serve various owners for almost 30 years. She finally sunk in Erie Harbor after being renamed the *Hunter Willis.*

<u>**From the October 8, 1893 Detroit Free Press:**</u>

HANGING IN THE SHROUDS
PERILOUS POSITION OF THE CREW OF THE WRECKED STEWART.
HEROIC RESCUE BY THE CAPTAIN AND CREW OF THE LOUISE.
THE IDA M. TORRENT BURNED TO THE WATER'S EDGE.
Flotsam and Jetsam of the Gales on the Lakes.

Capt. Titus and the crew of the schooner David Stewart, seven persons all told, reached the city at a late hour last night, and were seen by a Free Press reporter. Capt. Titus related briefly but clearly the story of the loss of his vessel.

The Stewart had got but a short distance below the dummy Friday morning, when she encountered the gale, which came from the southeast. It blew so violently that the vessel was turned back and run into Pigeon Bay for shelter, coming to anchor about two miles below Leamington, and perhaps a mile and a half from shore. There she lay safely until early in the afternoon, when the wind suddenly whipped around to the southwest with increased violence. The Stewart was thus caught in the bight of the bay, and her only hope of escape was to hold on to her anchors and ride out the gale. As darkness approached, the violence of the gale increased, and the terrific seas began to sweep the vessel's deck. By 9 o'clock Friday night it became evident that she could not much longer live under the immense bodies of water which now constantly deluged her decks. About this time the small boat was washed from the davits, leaving the crew no means of reaching shore. It was from the Stewart's name being painted on the yawl that the people on shore knew yesterday morning what vessel it was.

Between 10 and 11 o'clock Capt. Titus went forward to see how the anchors were holding, and while there saw that she was about to go down. He hastily jumped into the fore-rigging; the crew, who were all aft, at the same time clambered up the mizzen. The vessel seemed unable to free herself of the water, which filled her decks, and she foundered there at her anchors, going down in about thirty feet of water. The crew clung to their perilous position, expecting every moment that the spars would go out. Capt. Titus says that before they were taken off the mizzenmast was swaying in a most dangerous manner, and thinks it would not have stood much longer. At daylight yesterday the wreck was seen by people on shore, but there was no lifeboat in the vicinity, or any other means available for reaching the crew,

Most fortunately the fishing tug Louise, of Sandusky, was lying sheltered on the east side of the point, about opposite to where the Stewart was sunk. Information of the peril the crew was in was conveyed by fishermen on shore to the captain of the Louise who without a moment's hesitation got boat under way and ran around by the dummy to the wreck, where, with a great deal of difficulty, all were safely taken on board. As the sea was too heavy to permit a landing being made at Leamington, the Louise at once steamed for Sandusky, from which place Capt. Titus and his crew came to this city. All were greatly exhausted by their eleven hours exposure in the vessel's rigging. But will doubtless be all right in a few days.

The Wreck Today:

This wreck lies flattened in shallow silty water. Watch for heavy boat traffic.

GEORGE STONE

Official #: 86261   **Site #:** 78

Location: 4 miles west of Point Pelee on Grubbs Reef

Coordinates: LORAN: 43819.9   57135.0   DGPS: 41 53.249   82 33.248

Lies: bow east   **Depth:** 35 feet

Type: wood propeller   **Cargo:** coats & coal

Power: triple expansion engine, 2 scotch boilers

Owner(s) M. A. Bradley of Cleveland, Ohio

Built: 1893 at West Bay City, Michigan by F. W. Wheeler & Company

Dimensions: 270' x 40' x 19'1"   **Tonnage:** 1841.22 gross 1501.65 net

Date of Loss: Wednesday, October 13, 1909

Cause of Loss: storm & fire

George Stone
Great Lakes Historical Society

Story of the Loss:

A southwest gale was blowing as the *Stone* made her way upbound from Ashtabula, Ohio toward Racine, Wisconsin. About 10:00 p.m. she struck Grubbs Reef and wired for help. Due to the severity of the storm, the pumps had already been hard at work. Several vessels passed, either missing the sound of the *Stone's* whistle, or fearing for their own safety. In the midst of the chaos, a lamp was knocked over, igniting the pilothouse, which burned until the high seas extinguished the flames.

After the pumps failed, the captain ordered a wooden lifeboat launched. It was promptly smashed. However, Captain Howell and 7 crewmen were able to leave the steamer in a metal lifeboat. Five crewmen perished when the lifeboat overturned. Captain Howell and two crewmembers made it to shore. However, the captain did not survive.

Two hours later, Captain Fred Dupuy of the *F. M. Osborne* rescued ten crewmen left on board. As the *Osborne* pushed her bow against the afterdeck of the stricken *Stone*, it was only "masterful seamanship" by Captain Dupuy that saved the *Stone's* remaining crew.

The Wreck Today:

Because the *Stone* was salvaged, much of her machinery is missing. Located on Grubbs Reef, there is a boiler on the port side. Notable features are her propeller, anchor chain, and anchor. Fish are abundant on this wreck. Save Ontario Shipwrecks (SOS) has placed a plaque and mooring on this site.

In 1997 SOS returned a number of artifacts to the *George Stone* and placed a monument commemorating sailor's lost lives. In 1999 a steel vessel was deliberately sunk next to the *George Stone*. Winter ice has reportedly shifted it to a position against the starboard bow of the *Stone*.

Watch for snagged fish nets and heavy boat traffic.

SUCCESS

Official #:	**Site #:** 93

Location: ½ mile off Port Clinton, Ohio

Coordinates: LORAN: 43616.4 56855.9   DGPS: 41 31.321 82 54.705

Lies:	bow southwest	**Depth:**	15 feet
Type:	teak barquentine	**Cargo:**	light
Power:	sail		
Owner(s)	Walter Kolbe of Port Clinton		
Built:	1840 in Moulmein, India by the British		
Dimensions:	135' x 30' x 14'	**Tonnage:**	621
Date of Loss:	Thursday, July 4, 1946		
Cause of Loss:	fire/grounding		

Success
Great Lakes Historical Society

Story of the Loss:

Much of the *Success's* "history" appears to have been invented by Joseph Harvie, an Australian who traveled as a showman exhibiting her as a "Convict Ship", **"The Last of England's Infamous Felon Fleet,"** in the United Kingdom and, the United States.

The *Success* was built of Burmese teak in India in 1840, not 1790 as was claimed by Harvie. For the first eight years of her life she was engaged in trade between England and the East Indies. She probably made her first trip to Australia in 1848. Although convicts were carried to New South Wales, the *Success* carried immigrants. Between 1848 and 1852, she carried settlers on several voyages between London and Australia. After her crew abandoned her to go to the gold fields in 1852, the Victorian government bought her for use as a prison.

An Australian government investigation, which refutes some of the make believe history, does not deny that inhumane practices were rampant during the ships use as a men's prison. In 1857, a party of prisoners killed their chief captor, Captain Price, and brought some of the abuses to light.

From 1860 to 1869 the *Success* was used to incarcerate women and boys. Subsequently, the ship was used to store ammunition.

In 1885, the *Success* was scuttled in the harbor at Sidney. She remained underwater for five years until she was raised to be used as a convict hulk ship exhibition. After exhibits in Australian waters, her owners took her to Great Britain and Ireland, where she remained from 1895 to 1912.

In 1912, the *Success* was bought by an American, Captain W. H. Smith who changed her rig and sailed her from Liverpool on the same day the *Titanic* left Southampton. After 96 days at sea, the half starved crew arrived with much fanfare in Boston. People flocked to see the old prison ship with her lurid, half-invented history. For 20 years, she visited ports on the east coast and Mississippi River. At one time, she traveled the Panama Canal to visit San Francisco. Ultimately, she was brought to the Great Lakes to spend the last of her days.

Her last owner, Walter Kolbe, acquired her in 1943 after she sank in Sandusky Bay. He said vandals made off with her teak figurehead, the likeness of an early English queen.

Walter Kolbe had purchased the *Success* to exhibit. However, due to her 14' draft, he was unable to bring the ship into Port Clinton from Sandusky. Instead, the *Success* lay east of the harbor. Her valuable teak wood was being recovered when a fire of unknown origin swept the ship late in the afternoon of July 4th 1946. The final act of this one time prison ship was to provide an Independence Day spectacle for holiday travelers along the coast road.

The Wreck Today:

Considering how shallow the water is at this site, a lot remains of the wreck. The spine and ribs rise 8 feet off the bottom and many fish use the remaining structure as their habitat. Parts of the wreck and metal fittings are still found in the sand and mud bottom. Watch for heavy boat traffic.

A deadeye and strap from the *Success* is at the Great Lakes Historical Society Museum in Vermilion, Ohio. Other artifacts are housed at the Rutherford B. Hayes Presidential Center in Fremont, Ohio.

Success ablaze on July 4, 1946. Author's collection.

TASMANIA

Official #:   75598   **Site #:**   67

Location: seven miles east of Pelee Island

Coordinates: LORAN: 43787.1 57140.3   DGPS: 41 47.303   82 29.811

Lies: bow west   **Depth:**   40 feet

Type: schooner   **Cargo:**   iron ore

Power: four masted Sail

Owner(s)   James Corrigan, Cleveland, Ohio

Built: 1871 at Port Huron, Michigan by Muir & Leighton

Dimensions: 221' x 35' x 16'   **Tonnage:**   979 gross 931 net

Date of Loss: Friday, October 20, 1905

Cause of Loss: foundered in a storm

Tasmania

Great Lakes Historical Society

Story of the Loss:

The *Tasmania* was formerly named *"James Couch"*.

Along with the barge *Ashland*, the *Tasmania* was under tow of the Steamer *Bulgaria*. They were en route from Escanaba, Michigan to Cleveland, Ohio when they encountered a huge storm that claimed 18 vessels and damaged 11 others on lakes Erie, Huron, and Michigan.

As the storm grew so intense that the crew of the *Bulgaria* could not see the *Ashland* or the *Tasmania*, the crew of the *Ashland* cut the towline to the *Tasmania*. The *Tasmania* seemed to founder almost at once. Captain William Radford and seven crewmen perished. Free of the drag of the *Tasmania*, the *Bulgaria* and *Ashland* were able to make the lee of Pelee Island and ride out the storm at anchor.

Two days later, the United States Assistant Engineer visited the sunken wreck. He found the 18 foot ensign floating attached to its halyards. It had been raised as a last, silent, appeal for help.

The Wreck Today:

In 1906, the wreck was dynamited to provide clearance for navigation. Her iron ore cargo forms a large mound. At the bow are two anchors, one of which was raised and later returned to the wreck. There is a capstan on the port side, a winch, and boiler. Well to the east of the wreck are the rudder and the wheel.

The bottom is sand with an occasional current.

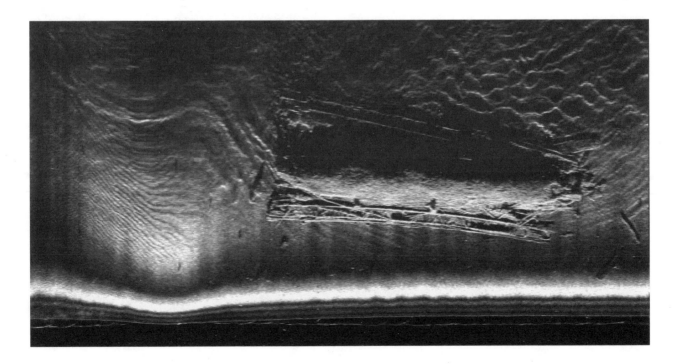

Sidescan image of the Tasmania.
Aqua Vision Research

TIOGA

Official #: 24167   **Site #:** 79

Location: 5 miles west of Pelee Point

Coordinates: LORAN: 43813.7   57116.1   DGPS: 41 53.032   82 35.353

Lies: bow east   **Depth:** 40 feet

Type: propeller   **Cargo:** barge tows

Power: vertical direct-acting engine

Owner(s) Captain C. C. Blodgett

Built: 1862 at Cleveland, Ohio by Quayle & Martin

Dimensions: 177.4' x 24.7' x 11.2'   **Tonnage:** 695

Date of Loss: Friday, October 5, 1877

Cause of Loss: fire

Tioga

Ralph Roberts' Collection

Story of the Loss:

The *Tioga* belonged directly or indirectly to the Erie Railroad until May of 1877. In April of 1864, she was cut by ice on a voyage from Cleveland to Dunkirk, New York and had to put into Erie, Pennsylvania. After Captain Blodgett purchased her from the Union Steam Boat Company, she became a steam lumber barge.

As she traveled upbound to Saginaw, Michigan, a fierce fall storm so discouraged the *Tioga* that she came to anchor with her tow barges slightly to the west of Pelee Point. About midnight a fire started near the boiler. The engineer attempted to smother the flames with steam from the boilers. However, the intense heat prevented anyone from getting close enough to effectively fight the fire. The high winds of the storm fanned the flames to an uncontrollable fury that could not be contained. Abandoning hope of saving their ship, the crew escaped to the barges and the propeller *Badger State* took off the *Tioga* captain. On October 6th the burned hulk sank. Three insurance companies covered most of the declared value of $15,000.

The Wreck Today:

The *Tioga* is located on a sand and mud bottom. There is a large boiler, but the engine is gone. She has a four blade prop. Look for the capstan by the rudder and the windlass forward.

TOLEDO

Official #:

Site #: 94

Location: 1 mile west of Rattlesnake Island

Coordinates: LORAN: 43690.7 56916.6   DGPS: 41 41.142   82 52.603

Lies: north/south, in three sections   **Depth:** 35 feet

Type: dredge   **Cargo:** stone

Power: towed

Owner(s) La Beau Wrecking Company, Captain Clarence La Beau of Toledo

Built:

Dimensions: **Tonnage:**

Date of Loss: Wednesday, November 19, 1924

Cause of Loss: foundered

Toledo

Ralph Roberts' Collection

Story of the Loss:

The *Toledo* had been working on filling around the Perry's Monument at South Bass Island. She encountered high winds and heavy seas while being towed back to Toledo, her homeport, by the tug *Burley*. Captain Le Beau decided to return to South Bass. While attempting the turn, the barge began to sink. The captain and seven crewmembers were thrown off the barge. The *Burley* launched a lifeboat but it was about a half hour before all of the exhausted crew were safely aboard the *Burley*. Suffering from exposure, the men were taken to Put-in-Bay at South Bass Island.

The Wreck Today

Located on a rock bottom, part of the frame supporting her cranes is evident. While much of the hull is under the silt, her steel pontoons and firebox are visible. To the south of the wreck you will find the cable drums.

CAUTION: steel cable from the cranes drapes over this wreck.

Perry's Monument

Two Fannies

Official #: 24144   **Site #:** 35

Location: 5 miles north of Bay Village, Ohio

Coordinates: LORAN: 43773.0 57385.3   DGPS: 41 33.855 81 55.281

Lies: bow east   **Depth:** 60 feet

Type: three masted Bark   **Cargo:** Iron ore

Power: towed

Owner(s) Captain Alfred Miller (50%), Aldrich of Hillsdale & Baldwin of Kinosha

Built: 1862 at Pishtigo, Wisconsin by George O. Spear

Dimensions: 152' x 33' x 12'   **Tonnage:** 492.24 gross 467.63 net

Date of Loss: Sunday, August 10, 1890

Cause of Loss: sprung a leak in heavy seas

Two Fannies

Historical Collections of the Great Lakes

Story of the Loss:

Used primarily in the lumber trade, the *Two Fannies* carried iron ore when down bound. Rebuilt in 1876; originally 149'6' x 33'3" x 12'4".

Along with consorts *Commanche* and *Hallaran*, the *Two Fannies* left Escanaba, Michigan in tow of the tug *Crusader*. Her cargo of iron ore was consigned to M.A. Hanna Company in Cleveland, Ohio. Due to a two day long blow out of the northwest, her passage was rough all the way. The ride was uncomfortable, but safe, until they encountered the heavy chop that is so typical of Lake Erie. In Erie's notorious short waves, the *Two Fannies* sprung a leak. At 10:30 p.m. the lookout informed Captain Alfred Miller that water was rising rapidly in the hold. Despite immediately manning the pumps, the water rose five feet in three hours.

"I saw that she was going," said Captain Miller, "and hurried out the yawl boat. The entire crew, including myself, six men, and a woman cook, tumbled into the boat and pushed off. We were not a second too soon, for before we were fairly out of the schooners suction she heaved and went down with a rush." The following morning, the yawl was taken in tow by the steamer *City of Detroit*. Only two of the crew boarded the steamer. Shortly thereafter, the boats were met by the tug *James Amedeus*. The remaining five crewmembers boarded the tug and all were landed safely in Cleveland.

Another Fannie was a victim of the same storm. The *Fannie L. Jones* sunk off Cleveland with a load of stone.

The Wreck Today:

The *Two Fannies* lies upright in 60 feet of water. Her decking is gone and, while much of the stern is collapsed, her huge rudder and rudderpost are an impressive sight. The centerboard and bracing beams dominate the mid section of the wreck. Look for the windlass, chain, ships knees, occasional deadeyes, and two capstans.

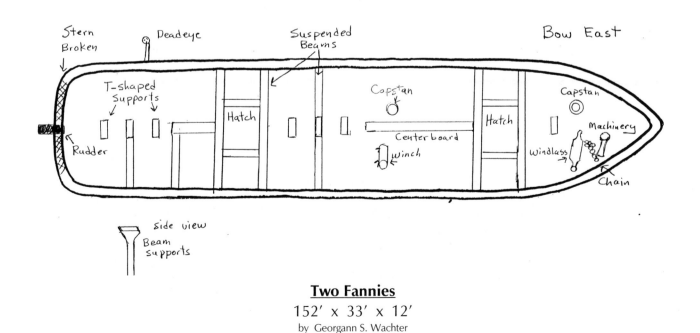

Two Fannies
152' x 33' x 12'
by Georgann S. Wachter
Not to scale

VALENTINE

Official #:	25732	**Site #:**	20
Location:	29 miles north-northeast of Avon Point, Ohio		
Coordinates:	LORAN: 43931.4 57476.3	DGPS: 41 55.116 81 54.778	
Lies:	bow north	**Depth:**	80 feet
Type:	schooner	**Cargo:**	stone
Power:	sail, three masted		
Owner(s)	Captain D. Miller of Toledo		
Built:	1867 at Conneaut, Ohio by P. White		
Dimensions:	128' x 25'8" x 10'	**Tonnage:**	271
Date of Loss:	Wednesday, October 10, 1877		
Cause of Loss:	foundered		

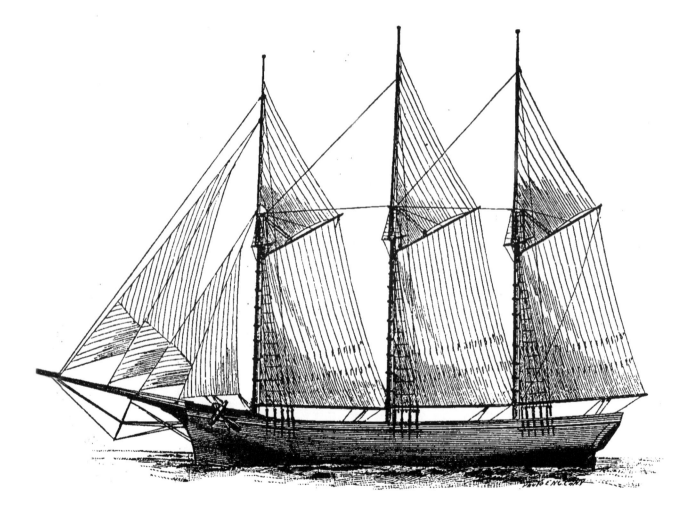

Typical Three Masted Schooner
Merchant Vesels of the US

Story of the Loss:

The *Valentine* went ashore in Port Austin in 1873.

The schooner *Valentine* foundered Wednesday night, October 10, 1877. The crew took to the boat with nothing but the clothing on their backs. After 16 hours hard labor, they landed east of Fairport Harbor, Ohio. One crewman was heard to tell the Cleveland Herald, "We were all well beat out, having had to work backing the boat all the way ashore."

The Wreck Today:

When this wreck site was first discovered a novice diver went down to investigate the find. He returned to the surface and reported there was nothing but a telephone pole sticking up. The more experienced divers aboard the boat that day scrambled to suit up and be the first to investigate a "virgin" wreck. They all knew that a telephone pole in the middle of Lake Erie could only be one thing, a ships mast!.

The *Valentine* is well preserved on the bottom. Although her anchors are removed, at the bow you will find the windlass, anchor chain, and pumps. As you move toward the stern, past the broken foremast, you find a winch, hold opening, and capstan. There is a second winch, the main mast base, and pump amidships and on the stern you'll find the rudder post and old hemp fish nets snared on the wreck.

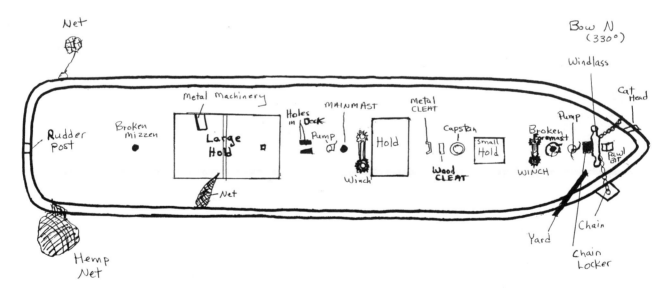

Valentine
128' x 25'8"' x 10'
by Georgann S. Wachter
Not to scale

DAVID VANCE

Official #: 6855   **Site #:** 72

Location: southwest of Pelee Point

Coordinates: LORAN: 43813.8   57144.3   DGPS: 41 51.726   82 31.438

Lies: bow south   **Depth:** 41 feet

Type: schooner   **Cargo:** coal

Power: three masted sail

Owner(s) James McKenzie of Buffalo, New York and Benjamin Budsell of Milwaukee, Wisconsin

Built: 1874 by J. Butler at Manitowoc, Wisconsin

Dimensions: 206'6" x 33'7" x 14'4"   **Tonnage:** 774.76 gross   736.03 net

Date of Loss: Thursday, July 20, 1893

Cause of Loss: collision

David Vance
Loudon Wilson Collection, Historical Collections of the Great Lakes

Story of the Loss:

Canadians call this location the "Wheel Wreck". In May of 1877, the *Vance* and the barge *Brunnette* collided in Pelee Passage. The port bow of the *Vance* was badly damaged. In 1886, the *David Vance* sank at Amherstburg but was recovered.

The *David Vance*, towed by the steamer *Samoa*, and the *Lizzie A. Law*, towed by the steamer *Egyptian*, collided when the steamers turned too sharply after passing in Pelee Passage. Captain Mason of the *Vance* had his wife and three young daughters aboard. The yawl boat was lowered and the two younger daughters and several crewmen boarded the small vessel. Mrs. Mason had to jump into the water and was rescued, with difficulty, by the mate. Captain Mason, with his oldest daughter in his arms, jumped into the lake. They were taken aboard the yawl. The remaining crew floated in the water until they were picked up by the *Samoa*.

The *Lizzie A. Law* also sank but was salvaged only to eventually sink in Lake Superior.

An unsuccessful salvage attempt was made on the *Vance* in October of 1893.

The Wreck Today:

Located on a sand bottom, the *Vance* is flattened. There is a centerboard, ships wheel, deadeyes, and rudder post. Several hundred yards west of the site is the wreck of the *Charger*.

Bracketed between a steamer & her consort is the schooner **Lizzie Law**, *which sunk in Pelee Passage after striking the* **David Vance**. *Authors collection.*

FRANK E. VIGOR

Official #: 116732   **Site #:** 19
Location: 30 miles north of Avon Point in the shipping lanes & Canadian waters
Coordinates: LORAN: 43942.0 57464.4   DGPS: 41 57.545   81 57.242
Lies: bow north   **Depth:** 90 feet
Type: propeller   **Cargo:** sulfur
Power: 1,800 HP triple expansion engine 21"-41"-66"x42"
Owner(s) Columbia Transportation Company, Cleveland, Ohio
Built: 1896, Globe Iron Works, Cleveland, Ohio   Hull #67
Dimensions: 418'3" x 48'2" x 23'9"   **Tonnage:** 4067 gross 3143 net
Date of Loss: Thursday, April 27, 1944
Cause of Loss: collision with *Philip Minch*

Frank E. Vigor
Great Lakes Historical Society

Story of the Loss:

Launched July 25, 1896 as the bulk freighter *Sir William Siemans*, she was renamed *William B. Pilkey* in 1929. In 1942, under her final owners, she was converted to a crane ship at Fairport Machine Shop, Fairport, Ohio, and renamed *Frank E. Vigor*. She was originally built as a bulk freighter at 4344 gross tons and 3293 net.

At about 10:00 a.m., while traveling in a heavy fog, the *Vigor* collided with the *Philip Minch*. The *Minch* struck the *Vigor's* starboard side about 100 feet from the stern. Signals were given to abandon ship and the lifeboat was lowered as the *Minch* held the dying *Vigor* from capsizing. Three of the crew were unable to board the overloaded lifeboat. They were tossed into the air as the ship settled on her starboard side and sank. George Bacon, one of the unlucky three tossed into the water stated, "When I opened my eyes above the water, I saw food, clothing, chairs, oil, and all sorts of things floating on the surface." The three crewmen were rescued by the *Philip Minch* and, along with two crewmen from the *Minch,* were treated at a hospital in Lorain, Ohio.

In another part of the fog shrouded lake, two other steamers, the *James H. Reed* and *Ashcroft*, also collided, sinking the *Reed* and taking nine men and one woman to their deaths.

The Wreck Today:

The *Vigor* is upside down in the mud. She lays basically north/south with the bow to the north. One of her cranes lies 70 feet off to the east near the bow. Along with the vents, the cargo of sulfur is scattered on the port side (east).

Her engine room access hatch is blown off and the wreck may be entered at this point. **CAUTION:** This is a very dangerous penetration. Cables and machinery block the area and are suspended precariously from above. Even for a careful diver, once you are inside, the wreck silts up instantly reducing visibility to zero. Only very experienced divers with appropriate training and equipment for shipwreck penetration should consider entering this wreck.

Damage to the Philip Minch following the collision. Photo from Great Lakes Historical Society, Bowen Collection

ANTHONY WAYNE

Official #:   **Site #:**   51

Location: 8 miles north of Vermillion, Ohio

Coordinates: sorry, still secret

Lies: scattered   **Depth:**   60 feet

Type: sidewheel steamer   **Cargo:**   passengers, pork lard, seeds,
                                                                   butter, & barrels of whiskey

Power: 28' diameter paddle wheels

Owner(s)   Charles B. Howard & Company of Detroit, Michigan

Built: 1837 at Perrysburg, Ohio by Samuel Hubbell

Dimensions: 155' x 27'4" x 10'   **Tonnage:**   400 80/95

Date of Loss: Sunday, April 28, 1850

Cause of Loss: explosion

Anthony Wayne
Great Lakes Historical Society

Story of the Loss:

Launched as the *General Wayne*. The name was changed to *Anthony Wayne* in 1839. In 1848 she was involved in an accident and sold. She was extensively rebuilt in Trenton, Michigan in 1849. This rebuild included two new boilers.

The *Anthony Wayne* left Toledo, Ohio for Buffalo, New York with 60 passengers and crew on April 27, 1850. She made a stop in Sandusky, where she took on approximately 40 more passengers. As she steamed north of Vermilion, shortly after midnight April 28th, both boilers exploded. Scalding water injured several people and fire was spreading rapidly in the deck areas of the stricken vessel.

Two boats were launched. The yawl boat, under command of the mate, headed for the schooner *Elmina*, while a raft containing the captain and three others pulled to shore. In fifteen minutes, the *Wayne* sank, separating the hurricane deck from the rest of the ship. Several survivors clung to this makeshift raft until the *Elmira* rescued them at daybreak.

Mr. Archer Brackney, traveling with his daughter and son, plunged into the water after the explosion. Searching in the water for something to float on, he spotted the coffin of his deceased wife and child. He placed his living children on the coffin, but in the waves, his son fell off and perished.

On reaching shore, Captain Gore sounded the alarm and the steamer *Islander* put out and towed the *Elmina*, which had picked up many survivors and corpses, to shore. As is often the case, reports of the number of people on board and the total loss of life vary from one account to another. It is estimated that 100 people were on board. Eleven crewmembers perished in the incident and between 40 and 50 passengers.

The Wreck Today:

In 1991 two local wreck hunters petitioned for rights to salvage the gold purported to be on board (it isn't on the manifests and no one who has dove it owns up to finding any). To our knowledge, no action was ever taken on the request.

The wreckage of the *Wayne* is spread over a large area with the bow and stern exposed. Her sidewheels are flat and one is entirely burried in the silt.

Wend the Wave

Official #:   26836   **Site #:**   62

Location: just east of Point Pelee

Coordinates: LORAN: 43829.2   57174.3   DGPS: 41 52.912   82 28.532

Lies: bow north   **Depth:**   30 feet

Type: schooner/barge   **Cargo:**   coal

Power: sail or tow

Owner(s)   Hern & Hollywood of Bay City, Michigan

Built: 1867 by Rugby at Ashtabula, Ohio

Dimensions: 128′ x 28′ x 10′   **Tonnage:**   250.13 gross 239 net

Date of Loss: Sunday, October 6, 1889

Cause of Loss: collision with the *J. D. Sawyer* in storm

Windlass

On display at Port Huron Museum, Port Huron, Michigan
photo Georgann Wachter

Story of the Loss:

John Monk of Sandusky converted the *Wend the Wave* to a barge in 1882.

The *Wend the Wave* was under tow with the *A.W. Wright, Antelope,* and *Taylor*. The tow vessel, *Glasgow* was having difficulty in a northwest gale and ran aground on Point Pelee. The towed vessels anchored near the point. Subsequently, the *J.D. Sawyer* ran into the *Wend the Wave* at the cabin. While the rest of the crew scrambled aboard the *Sawyer*, Captain Heron ran to the cabin to try and save his sister-in-law, the cook. He finally abandoned his vessel and, once aboard the *Sawyer*, tried to get Captain Clump of the *Sawyer* to return to the *Wend the Wave* to determine if cook, Kate McMann was killed in the collision. Captain Heron berated the captain of the *Sawyer* for not turning back.

When a U.S. Marshal attempted to detain he *Sawyer* for sinking the *Wend the Wave*, Captain Clump was almost arrested for threatening the marshal with a handspike.

Captain Clump maintained that no anchor lights were showing on the barge, but the crews of all four barges maintained they were lit.

The Wreck Today:

The *Wend the Wave* lays flattened on a sand bottom and sand and zebra mussels cover much of the wreck. There is a windlass, small section of wood, and two boxlike structures we believe to be the mast steps. All else appears to have been buried beneath the sand bottom.

Watch for heavy boat traffic.

WESSEE

Official #:   US155401 Can138574   **Site #:**   100

Location: Middle Sister Island.

Coordinates: LORAN: 43739.4 56895.1   DGPS: 41 50.592 82.59.567

                                               PROP SHAFT: 41 50.609 82 59.850

Lies: bow south/southwest   **Depth:**   22 feet

Type: wood propeller   **Cargo:**

Power: fore and aft compound engine

Owner(s)   R. Massey and William Gatfield of Sandwich, Ontario (Burder Transit Company)

Built: 1901 at Greenbay, Wisconsin by Andrew Johnson

Dimensions: 265'5" x 42' x 22'7"   **Tonnage:**   1829 gross 1062 net

Date of Loss: Monday, November 12, 1923

Cause of Loss: fire

Wessee
Historical Collections of the Great Lakes

Story of the Loss:

Originally launched as the *Orion*, she became the *Wesee* when she was rebuilt in Manitowoc, Wisconsin in 1917. She was sold to Canadian interests in 1920 and remeasured.

The *Wesee* caught fire about midnight and was beached on Middle Sister Island. The crew of 18 men and the woman cook escaped in two yawl boats.

Landing on the island, they encountered two starving fishermen from Port Clinton, Ohio who had been marooned for 4 ½ days. The fishermen had been transporting a cabin cruiser from Sandwich, Ontario to Port Clinton, Ohio when it sprang a leak. The shipwrecked sailors from Port Clinton had lit a fire and scavenged 4 onions, an apple, and a radish. This is all they had eaten since landing on the 20 acre island. The November 13th *Toledo Blade* tells their story as follows:

> Friday Bossom and Bass (the stranded boaters) made a circuit of the island, which contains about 20 acres, and found four onions, one radish and one apple washed up on the beach. From these they made a broth, but it was rather weak and didn't last long. When their cigarette supply was exhausted the men smoked home made ones of dried leaves rolled in pieces of newspaper. They kept the fire burning night and day but saw no boats. The island is not on any of the lake routes. Part of the time the air was misty. There were plenty of ducks about the island the fishermen said but they had no guns and their efforts at stalking were unsuccessful. There was not the slightest trace of a fish line or hook on the island and they could find nothing with which to improvise a hook. As a last resort the men decided to patch up the leak in the power boat as best they could, although there were no tools or materials with which to work. It was planned to rig up a sail with in old strip of canvass and a piece of driftwood and push off.

Fortunately, the steamer, *Conneaut* had spotted the flames of the *Wesee* and she rescued all of the sailors, probably saving the lives of the two men from Port Clinton.

Eventually, the cabin cruiser was recovered and delivered to her owner.

The Wreck Today:

The *Wesee* lays scattered on the rocks south of Middle Sister. Large frame members and metal parts remain. Her engine and boilers were removed. The propeller and shaft lie off the main wreckage.

M.I. Wilcox

Official #:   17617   **Site #:**   98
Location: 2000 feet southwest from Colchester, Ontario dock
Coordinates: LORAN: 43802.2   56959.5   GPS: 41 58.83   82 56.45
Lies: bow south   **Depth:**   22 feet
Type: schooner   **Cargo:**   coal
Power: sail, three masted
Owner(s)   C. Baumhart of Vermilion, Ohio
Built: 1866 at Toledo, Ohio by Bailey Brothers
Dimensions: 137 x 27'5" x 12'7"   **Tonnage:**   377 gross 358 net
Date of Loss: Tuesday, May 8,1906
Cause of Loss: sprung a leak anchored in a gale

M. I. Wilcox

Historical Collections of the Great Lakes

Story of the Loss:

The *M.I. Wilcox* was one of several vessels named foe Minot Ignatius Wilcox, a shipbuilder and owner of a steam dredge firm.

While anchored riding out a gale near Colchester, the aging *Wilcox* began to leak. The pumps were unable to contain the flow, so the crew of five took to the yawl boat. Once ashore, they wandered through the darkness until they found shelter in a nearby farmhouse.

Lost in this same storm were the schooners *Algeria*, and *Iron Queen* off Cleveland and the schooner *Armenia* west of Point Pelee.

The Wreck Today:

The hull is split open on this shallow wreck. Scattered along the wreckage, you will find the windlass, capstan, deadeyes, wheel, winches, and anchor. Off the stern are an anchor and a donkey boiler. The rudder and wheel lie off the starboard side.

Many bass call this wreck home.

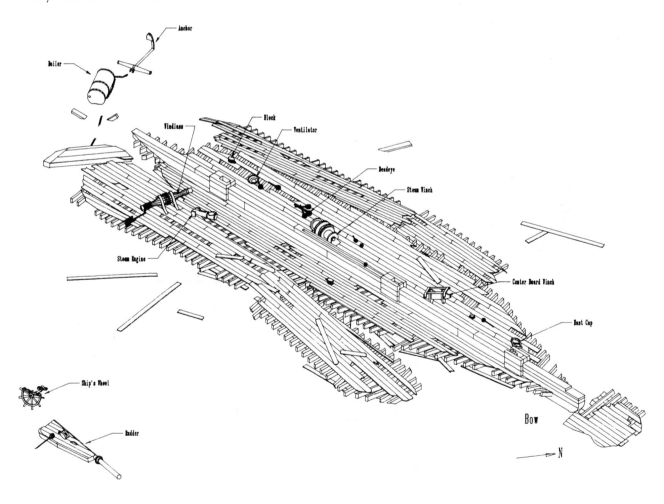

1993 site survey compliments of Save Ontario Shipwrecks .

WILLIS

Official #:   none   **Site #:**   55

Location: 20 miles north of Lorain, Ohio

Coordinates: LORAN: 43897.7   57349.8   DGPS: 41 55.874   82 09.658

Lies: bow northeast   **Depth:**   75 feet

Type: schooner   **Cargo:**   iron ore

Power: sail, three masted

Owner(s)   J.R. Slauson & Captain William Pugh of Racine, Wisconsin

Built: 1872 by Peter Larson in Manitowoc, Wisconsin

Dimensions: 131'7" x 27'9" x 9'   **Tonnage:**   245

Date of Loss: Monday, November 11, 1872

Cause of Loss: collision

Willis

Painting by Peter Rindlesbacker courtesy of Roy Pickering, owner

Story of the Loss:

First enrolled May 14, 1872, the *Willis* had a very short life on the lakes. She sank in her maiden year!

Brand new to the lake, the *Willis* was proud and beautiful with a carvel hull design, three masts, and two unique tear drop shaped portholes on her plum stern. Downbound from Escanaba, Michigan she carried iron ore when she collided with the bark *Elizabeth Jones*. The collision left he *Jones* undamaged but the *Willis*, stove in on her starboard quarter, sank quickly.

The Wreck Today:

Sitting upright in 72 feet of water, the *Willis* is one of the most impressive wrecks in western Lake Erie. Her bow sprint reaches majestically to the east as though still longing to complete her voyage. Several deadeyes and blocks remain and two masts lay fallen to starboard. While divers have removed much of the rigging, the steering gear, capstan, and windlass are intact. Be sure to drop over the stern and see the key hole openings where her unique portholes were mounted.

*The **Willis** is shown as she lies underwater in this Peter Rindlesbacker painting.*
Courtesy Roy Pickering, owner

MABEL WILSON

Official #: 91872   **Site #:** 30

Location: ½ mile west of the Cleveland lighthouse

Coordinates: LORAN: 43774.3 57470.5   DGPS: 41 30.342 81 43.907

Lies: north-south   **Depth:** 36 feet

Type: schooner   **Cargo:** iron ore

Power: sail, four masted

Owner(s) P.J. Ralph and Company of Detroit, Michigan

Built: 1886 at West Bay City, Michigan by F.W. Wheeler and Company

Dimensions: 242'9" x 39'2" x 16'2"   **Tonnage:** 1224.58 gross 1185.15 net

Date of Loss: Monday, May 28, 1906

Cause of Loss: sprung a leak

Mabel Wilson
Historical Collections of the Great Lakes

Story of the Loss:

James Gotham and his older brother, Emdoubleyew Gotham, were both captains. Emdoubleyew had forsaken sailing vessels for the *Silvanus J. Macy*, a steamer that often towed the *Mabel Wilson*. On November 22, 1902, the two vessels cleared Buffalo. A southwest gale blew up and the *Macy* cast off the *Wilson* in mid lake. The *Mabel Wilson* battled for four days to reach Detroit, where James Gotham learned that the *Silvanus J. Macy* had foundered, taking his brother and crew to their deaths.

Under the command of Captain James Gotham, the *Wilson* left Escanaba, Michigan with a full load of iron ore. The propeller *C.W. Elphicke* towed her. After entering Lake Erie, she took shelter in Pigeon Bay for a while as a north gale was blowing. When the wind changed to the northeast, the vessel proceeded to Cleveland. At 1:30 a.m. the crew informed Captain Gotham she had sprung a leak. The men pumped furiously but the water gained on them. The *Elphicke* towed the waterlogged vessel to the Cleveland Harbor entrance and whistled for a tug. Before the tug *Lutz* could reach the *Wilson*, the *Elphicke* cut loose and the *Wilson* wallowed in the heavy seas. On three separate attempts by the *Lutz* to pick up the towline, the line broke. The lifesaving station was alerted and Captain Motley and his crew (oh wow, a motley crew) set out in a small boat.

Three of the *Wilson's* crewmen climbed the rigging as she suddenly sank, throwing timbers and hatch covers into the air. One seaman, known only as Fred, had been hanging on a boom that broke off. Before the *Lutz*, who rescued three men, or the lifesavers could reach him; Fred was gone to the deep. Captain Motley and his crew had rescued four men when the debris holed their lifeboat. They were picked up by the tug *William Kennedy*. Captain Gotham and two other injured sailors were taken to the marine hospital.

In October of 1913, the *C.W. Elphicke* became a casualty of the lake when she grounded on Long Point.

The Wreck Today:

Although the wreck was dynamited, a portion of the stern remains intact. Her debris field is extensive. Visibility at this location is often very limited.

CAUTION: There is heavy boat traffic in this area because of a nearby marina.

GEORGE WORTHINGTON

Official #: 10223   **Site #:** 96

Location: off Colchester Reef, Ontario

Coordinates: LORAN: 43800.0   56994.4   DGPS: 41 56 675   82 51 326

Lies: **Depth:** 38 feet

Type: schooner   **Cargo:** coal

Power: sail, two masted

Owner(s) Captain W. E. Rice, Detroit, Michigan

Built: 1852 by William Treat at Euclid Creek, Ohio

Dimensions: 119'9" x 25'2" x 10'1"   **Tonnage:** 231 gross 219 net

Date of Loss: Saturday, July 23, 1887

Cause of Loss: collision

Story of the Loss:

Rebuilt in 1887, the *George Worthington* was being towed by the steam barge *Mackinac*. The weather was stormy, and the schooner *George W. Davis* was running free with the winds. The *Mackinac* steamed across the path of the onrushing *Davis*, pulling the *Worthington* into harms way. Captain Martin Elnan of the schooner *George W. Davis* claimed he made the proper signals but the *Mackinac* ignored these, as she pulled the *Worthington* in front of the *Davis*. The *Worthington* sank shortly after the collision with the *George W. Davis*.

The *Worthington's* crew launched boats and were picked up by the *Davis*. The tug *Wilcox* towed the damaged *Davis* to Amherstberg, Ontario and then on to Fairport, Ohio for repairs.

Captain Elnan went on to be skipper of the *Dundee* and barely survived her sinking in September of 1900.

The Wreck Today:

There are two wood stock anchors connected to the windlass, deadeyes, centerboard, and winch. You'll find tools at the stern and some fishnet snagged at the bow.

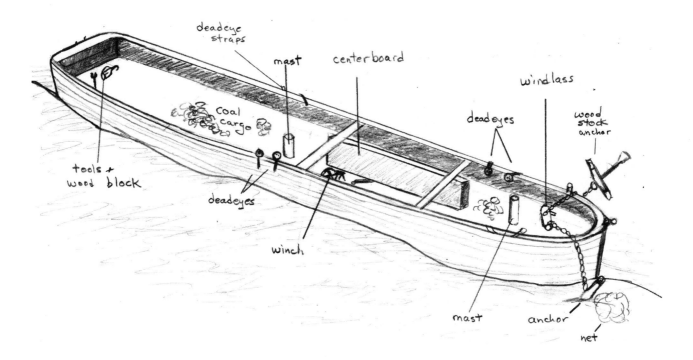

deadeye straps

mast

centerboard

windlass

wood stock anchor

deadeyes

Coal cargo

tools + wood block

deadeyes

winch

mast

anchor

net

George Worthington
119' x 25'2"' x 10'1"
by Georgann S. Wachter
Not to scale

BIBLIOGRAPHY

BOOKS

Barrett, Harry B., ed. <u>Lakelore</u>. London, Ontario: Fanshawe College, 1973.

Berent, John. <u>Diving the Lake Erie Island Wrecks</u>. Marblehead, Ohio: published by the author, 1992.

Bowen, Dana T. <u>Shipwrecks of the Lakes</u>. Cleveland, Ohio: Freshwater Press, 1952.

<u>Diving in Ohio</u>. Rootstown, Ohio: Ohio Council of Skin and Scuba Divers, Inc., 1976.

Greenwood, John O. <u>Namesakes 1910 - 1919</u>. Cleveland, Ohio: Freshwater Press, Inc., 1986.

Greenwood, John O. <u>Namesakes 1900 - 1909</u>. Cleveland, Ohio: Freshwater Press, Inc., 1987.

Harold, Steve. <u>Shipbuilding at Manistee</u>. Manistee, Michigan: published by the author, 1976

Havinghurst, Walter. <u>Long Ships Passing</u>. New York, McMillan Company, 1944.

Heyl, Eric. <u>Early American Steamers, Vols I - VI</u>. Buffalo, New York: published by the author at 136 West Oakwood Place, 1961 - 1969.

Heyden, Karl E. <u>Directory of Shipwrecks of the Great Lakes</u>. Boston: Bruce Humphries Publishers, 1966.

Inches, H. C. <u>The Great Lakes Wooden Shipbuilding Era</u>. Vermilion, Ohio: The Great Lakes Historical Society, 1976.

Kohl, Cris. <u>Dive Southwestern Ontario!</u>. Chatham, Ontario: published by the author, 1985.

Kohl, Cris. <u>Dive Ontario Two! More Ontario Shipwreck Stories</u>. Chatham, Ontario: published by the author, 1994.

Kohl, Cris. <u>Dive Ontario</u>. Chatham, Ontario: published by the author, 1990 revised 1995.

Lane, Kit. <u>Built on the Banks of the Kalamazoo, Book 1</u>. Douglas, Michigan: Pavilion Press, 1993.

Lauer, Rich. <u>Freshwater Vision</u>. Reynoldsburg, Ohio: Subaquatics, Inc. 1989.

Lytle, William. <u>Merchant Steam Vessels of the U.S. 1807 - 1868</u>. Mystic, Connecticut: Steamship Historical Society of America, 1952.

Meakin, Alexander C. <u>The Story of the Great Lakes Towing Company</u>. Vermillion, Ohio: The Great Lakes Historical Society, 1984.

Merchant Vessels of the U.S. (various years). Washington: Government Printing Office.

Prothero, Frank and Nancy. Tales of the North Shore. Port Stanley, Ontario: Nan-Sea Publications, 1987.

Submerged Cultural Resources Study. Leamington, Ontario: Corporation of the Town of Leamington, 1995.

Swayze, David D. Shipwreck!. Boyne City, Michigan: Harbor House Publications, Inc., 1992.

Tiessen, Ron. Shipwrecks, Pelee Island, and the Life Saving Service. Pelee Island Heritage Center, 1992

Van der Linden, Rev. Peter J., ed. and the Marine Historical Society of Detroit. Great Lakes Ships We Remember. Cleveland, Ohio: Freshwater Press, 1979 revised 1984.

Wendt, Gordon. In the Wake of the Walk-in-the-Water. Sandusky, Ohio: Commercial Printing Co., 1984

PERIODICALS

Cross, E. R. "Technifacts" *Skin Diver Magazine*, September 1988.

Kohl, Cris. "Lake Erie's Lost Steamers: The Colonial", *Great Lakes Diver Magazine*, April/May 1995.

Many articles from newspapers throughout the Great Lakes region were used to gather data for this book.

MISCELLANEOUS

"Master Sheets", Historical Collections of the Great Lakes, Bowling Green State University, Bowling Green, Ohio for the following vessels: Adventure, Algeria, Armenia, Isabella Boyce, Marshall F. Butters, Cascade, Case, City of Concord, Clarion, H. G. Cleveland, James B. Colgate, Colonel Cook/Augusta, Colonial, Conemaugh, Cortland, Craftsman, George Dunbar, S.F. Gale, Jay Gould, Grand Traverse, Duke Luedtke, Lycoming, John B. Lyon, Magnet, Mecosta, Merida, F.A. Meyer, Phillip Minch, Amaretta Mosher, North Carolina, Charles B. Packard, John Pridgeon Jr., F. H. Prince, Queen of the West, Quito, James H. Reed, Sarah E. Sheldon, Charles Spademan, Specular, George Stone, Tasmania, Two Fannies, Frank E. Vigor, Wesee,Willis, Mable Wilson.

BIBLIOGRAPHY

PHOTOGRAPHS

In addition to pictures from our private collection, photographs for this publication were provided by:

Buffalo & Erie County Historical Society. Buffalo, New York.

Father Edward J. Dowling Collection. University of Detroit, Mercy Library. Detroit Michigan.

Great Lakes Historical Society. Vermilion, Ohio.

Al Hart. Bay Village, Ohio.

Historical Collections of the Great Lakes. Bowling Green State University. Bowling Green, Ohio.

Lower Lakes Marine Historical Society. Buffalo, New York.

Milan Historical Society. Milan, Ohio.

Gerry Duff Paine, Avon Lake, Ohio.

Ralph Roberts. Saginaw, Michigan.

Phyllis Ruetschle, West Salem, Ohio.

NEED ADDITIONAL COPIES?

Additional copies of **ERIE WRECKS WEST** and **ERIE WRECKS EAST**
may be ordered directly from the publisher:

Corporate Impact

33326 Bonnieview Drive, Suite 200
Avon Lake, Ohio 44012-1230

Phone: 440-930-2477
Fax: 440-930-2525
Email: impact@kellnet.com
www.ErieWrecks.com

Georgann and Mike Wachter have been diving around the world since the early 1970's. They discovered diving while snorkeling in the Mediterranean Sea in 1972 during a backpacking trip through Europe. Since that time, they have visited many sites in the Caribbean, Atlantic, Pacific, and Great Lakes. However, nowhere else in the world have they discovered the kind of pristine and perfectly preserved shipwrecks that lie in the fresh waters of the Great Lakes.

Living near Lake Erie led to the fascination with Lake Erie shipwrecks that drove the extensive research effort that is exhibited in **ERIE WRECKS EAST** and **ERIE WRECKS WEST**. Early on, guests diving aboard the Wachter's boat would ask about the details of a shipwreck while en route to the site. In order to answer these questions, Mike and Georgann began keeping a notebook on board that contained photos and information on many of the shipwrecks they were diving. This kept Mike from making up false stories to answer the many questions. As the notebook grew, many friends suggested that the book should be published. Once the decision was made to publish a book on Lake Erie shipwrecks, the real work began. What was once a part time hobby has become a full time investigation of the myths and realities behind the thousands of shipwrecks in the Great Lakes. The Wachters have published three books, and several magazine articles, but their work is only beginning. With over 2,000 ships known to have sunk in Lake Erie alone, we can look forward to many more articles, books, and shipwreck materials from this husband and wife team.

Georgann is an accomplished researcher who is sought after as a speaker on sport diving, Great Lakes shipwrecks, and aquatic life. Mike makes his living as a management consultant and public speaker. For both Georgann and Mike, their first love is shipwreck diving. The collaboration of Georgann's love of research and Mike's love of story telling provides the fuel for the Erie Wrecks series.